Dear Patty,

Another book about the Island. I hope you enjoy it as much as I have.

Love, Rick

First
Spring

First Spring

A MARTHA'S VINEYARD JOURNAL

by
Phyllis Méras

drawings by
Mary Lee Herbster

THE CHATHAM PRESS, INC. RIVERSIDE CONNECTICUT

FOR MY FATHER
AND TOM AND RICHARD

First printing March, 1972
Second printing August, 1972

Library of Congress Catalog Card Number: 77-184145
SBN 85699-042-6

Manufactured in the United States of America

Distributed by The Viking Press, Inc.

Contents

Epilogue in the Form of a Prologue

West Tisbury,
Martha's Vineyard, Mass.
May 3

My second spring here has begun, and my first year has ended. Again there are buds on the lilac bush and jonquils in gardens. The sun is painting shadows on the trees. The red-winged blackbirds are whistling, and now and then I hear Canada geese honking. I am told two of them have nested nearby—around the bend in the Parsonage Pond—and although I cannot see the nest, I see its occupants sometimes.

Yesterday I visited the Oak Bluffs School, and a first-grade boy had found some of that crate-packing material that comes in shreds and looks to me like a bird's nest. And it did to him, too, for he brought it into school to build a Baltimore oriole's nest. He had seen a Baltimore oriole's nest in a tree and wondered how it was put together.

I came here from New York to the *Vineyard Gazette,* a 125-year-old weekly admittedly, but agreeably, out of step with the times—a paper that is one of the last of its kind in America. There is no wire service, no job printing, no banner headlines. Its writing staff is four or five. For the last half century, its editors have been the Pulitzer Prize winner and conservationist, Henry Beetle Hough, and his wife, Elizabeth, who together fashioned a paper whose concerns are good news rather than bad and the Island instead of the world.

The *Gazette* office, in a weathered, shingle house two centuries old, is eminently suited to its traditions. In the yard, wild roses tap at the windowpanes and blackberries are abundant. A neighborhood Siamese cat suns on the cellar door. Robins bob in the birdbath in spring.

Because Martha's Vineyard is an island seven miles off the Massachusetts coast, it is a somewhat protected place—still free of much of the over-mechanized, over-rushed world. At least it used to be—which is why I chose to come.

I came for bird songs and spring flowers and open fields with deer nibbling; clear blue waters speckled with white sails; the spring underfoot when I seek wild cranberries; pines soughing at East Chop. Yet, in the nature of man's approach to earth and air and water—three of the ancient, supposedly indestructible elements that we have learned so late are not indestructible at all—I may find that they are missing soon, or altered so I no longer know them. For earth can so easily be emptied of its richness!

Land cut into picturesque house lots is no longer land of slender pines and beach grass. Water polluted with oil and offal loses its sparkling blueness. In air clouded with dump smoke, the fragrance of flowers and grass is missing.

I do not want that, and I am fearful of the future.

Up-Island the other day, surveyors were out, and they

waved amiably as I drove by. But later I learned that they were readying land for a housing development. The developer was taking pains to give his roads appropriate Island names, after Vineyard fauna and old traditions, so there would be a touch of fetching nostalgia in them. But when the roads are built and blacktopped, the sentiment of the names will matter very little. And when the trees are down and the ranch houses up and the barbecues grilling steaks, the perfume of arbutus will not matter, and the trilling of pinkletinks will be lost in the laughter of cocktail voices.

It was not so long ago that Senator Edward M. Kennedy's car plunged from the bridge at Chappaquiddick. Before the tragedy, it was a peaceful, rustic spot. But now the bass fishermen who used to flee the cities in anticipation of the long, still nights and pink, still dawns at Chappaquiddick's East Beach—where stripers sheer the surf like silver arrows—find far less of their accustomed solitude.

An oil spill somewhere at sea a February ago trapped hundreds of birds that floated, drifted, swam in any way their blackened, coarsened, gluey feathers would allow them toward Island shores to die.

Almost every year now, they tell me, there is an oil spill of lesser or greater magnitude somewhere off this shore, and the globules slicken the waves and make unnatural calms.

When I walk the Gay Head beach, there is almost always a patch of tar-like substance stuck to a wing of driftwood. And of course, the beach is littered, too, with white plastic detergent bottles and red plastic submarines and styrofoam chunks among the glistening rocks.

On woodland walks I have always enjoyed the mystery a winding road offers around each bend, when twists and curves and swoops throw new prospects into view. And I have liked seeing endless hills and downs in the distance. But now, everywhere, the hills have begun to squirm with roads. Sometimes they go virtually nowhere. Sometimes they parallel an existing route. Sometimes the men-in-a-hurry who belong in the city and are somehow misplaced in the country have urged wider, straighter routes for more efficient travel from one end of the Island to the other. Or a developer has sought new roads to open up the hills for building plots. Or the state has offered inviting sums for road-widening or building or paving, so a town has jumped at the prospect of dollars and decided to build a road rather than "lose the loot" (the way I have heard it put).

Of course, it is true that a winding country road is not efficient, and lilacs in bloom at a crossroad are big and bulgy and may block an impatient driver's view. Big buses need roof-room, too, and overhanging branches make a disagreeable squeaking noise on bus tops. Motorcyclists also prefer a straight-away for safe travel.

This past fall and winter, I went on walks when the roadside sumac was crimson, poison ivy golden and oak leaves russet overhead, and, with cold weather limiting winter road building, when the snow was falling and frosting tree limbs, and there was an unearthly quiet in the air. And last month, there were frail pink mayflowers peeking from nesting places under the leaves. But today I have heard the rumble of the bulldozer on one of my favorite roads, and a truck laden with rocks has gone by—sure signs both that it is road-building time again, and the nesting mayflowers will be torn up for a wider, safer highway. Next year, I know, there will still be woodsy places where I will find Indian pipes and lady slippers, but how much longer? The people who know birds tell me there are fewer parula warblers because the trees that bear the furry moss for their nests have been cut down, and fewer robins because of insecticides.

The jet airport crisis has ended. The State Forest has been cut down to make way for a plane that, at best, is only serving a handful of summer people. But those in the know maintain that no matter how fierce the fight against this inroad of progress, the battle would have been lost because the federal government wanted a jet airport here for use in emergencies, when too many planes are stacked over Boston.

The deer always liked to browse in the airport underbrush, and one would see them, tawny noses quivering in spring, but there are very few since the underbrush was cut.

As I look back on it, this has been a busy time. The Vineyard is still more untouched than most resorts because— until the Kennedy affair, at least—one still found those who had never heard of its sandy shores. But it is changing with a rapidity that is breathtaking. Those who cherish its clear, starry skies at night, herring creeks where herring tantalize the bass, needle-carpeted pine forests and unbroken views over the berried hills, must work to save them.

There are still those who are concerned with this task, and that is another reason why this is a place worth being in, for people in so much of the country have given up the fight. At the Chilmark town meeting in February, a boat-launching ramp that would have made Menemsha's teeming harbor even more bustling was turned down, and the diesel buses that snort and career and exude sickening fumes were banned from the village's entrance road.

And tentatively, here and there, there have been efforts to enact zoning, A group of West Tisburyites, fearful that some of its townspeople's generally admirable, but in this case misplaced, fear of encroachment on individual rights could delay zoning indefinitely, formed a neighborhood covenant. By its terms, they promised not to alter the use of their land for more than a generation. And there have been generous gifts and leases of land with similar stipulations. The West Tisbury Congregational Church bestowed three acres on the town to be a bird and wildlife sanctuary.

The Friends of Tisbury have planted flower plots at busy corners, and promised substitute trees for householders willing to have unsightly Dutch-elm blighted stumps dug from their lawns. So that, for all my fears of the "progress" the next decade may bring here, there is still more hope.

Although I am a recent year-round resident here, I am a fourth generation summer visitor, which gives me a feeling of kinship beyond that of a newcomer. The Island is precious in my memories, as it is in the memories of so many others who moored their first sailboats in Oak Bluffs' little harbor; toddled among high-bush blueberries above the Lagoon; caught blowfish from the Edgartown wharf and eels off Menemsha docks.

Through the years, Vineyard tranquility has attracted artists and writers and actors seeking anonymity; doctors and lawyers and diplomats trying to escape their city telephones. And its own population combines descendants of whalers and trap fishermen with Indian harpooners, Portuguese sailors with cranberry-pickers and Yankee farmers. Since I have been here, we have often talked together about this and that—the summer people, the winter people and I—and I have jotted down what we have talked about. For I have wanted to document what life is here before it disappears—if it is to go.

My journal offers no stark, dramatic revelations. Much of it has appeared in one form or another in the pages of the *Gazette*. The only order it is in is the order of the seasons and of conversations and notable events. My one wish is that those who read it may come to share my desire that the Vineyard of clean bays and smooth white sands and bobwhites whistling will not be destroyed.

First Spring

Long a city dweller, I am trying to become a country dweller again. I am learning that I must apply myself to it. In the city I had gradually, callously I suppose, trained myself not to observe Harlem rats and files of cockroaches outside restaurant doors, weeping women on Eighth Avenue and blind men shaking bent tin cups. Hardly a helpful attitude in the face of misery, but a common one among city folk.

Studiedly I kept my eyes closed, except at certain familiar turns where I knew it was safe to open them. But now I am back in the country, and I must learn to keep them always open again.

I have been here less than a week, but I have already watched the alewives running at Herring Creek and quail scurrying across West Tisbury roads. Two bustled into the field by the parsonage, where we are living, just last night.

The day before yesterday, there were goldfinches outside the kitchen window, and at Gay Head I saw something goldfinch-sized, but with an elegant royal-blue neck. Heretofore, my bird watching has been restricted to New York Public Library pigeons, Central Park sparrows and West Side starlings—to such an extent that when someone spoke to me recently about common terns, I was mystified and wrote on my scratch pad, "Comintern."

In this new country phase of my life, I have learned that mockingbirds and Baltimore orioles are attracted by halved oranges, and guinea hens like the flavor of woodticks.

In the way of fish lore, I now know that swordfish are best sought in warm pockets in the ocean, and that today's swordfish is not nearly so hardy as his forebears were. Time was when swordfish prospered in fifty-degree water. Nowadays, an informant tells me, they superciliously demand an environment ten degrees warmer.

It was news to me, too, to hear that Massachusetts lobsters will have nothing to do with Maine lobster pots because the latter are rectangular instead of rounded and not nearly so roomy. Yesterday I was told (but I can't believe it!) that a quahaug can live to be twelve, but his growth will be stunted if he lives with too many other clams.

Woodticks, I have learned, prefer light to dark objects, and it is only brown wasps, not black ones, that sting.

I have discovered that skunk cabbages sprout hind-end-to, and that the fragile Island shadbush I see everywhere should, now that I am an Islander, be called wild pear or deerkill. I have seen my first bell-like wild blueberries in bloom.

There have been hawks swooping over Katama fields and clusters of polished crows. I understand if I am realy alert, I may catch sight of an otter splashing and puttering in James' Pond at Lambert's Cove or a raccoon recently imported to the Island.

It was news to me that skunks find snapping turtle eggs a great delicacy. It was news, too, that there is a heron colony at Little Neck on Cape Pogue.

Frequently, in the city, a tendency not to listen accompanies the inclination not to look, for the sounds of a city are rarely enjoyable—screeching brakes, thudding subways, the curses of cab drivers, roaring jet engines, honking horns, rattling construction machinery, buzzing blowtorches, transistor radios, funereal elevator music. So my ears must be tuned in again, too, for bird calls and sea sounds, the rustle of new leaves, the barking of dogs on a still night, church bells ringing the hours, the haunting bellow of a foghorn.

As for smells, there is no way, really, to turn them off in the metropolis (except, of course, when city germs cause clothespin nose). For six years, I have been smelling exhaust fumes and hot dog and sauerkraut stands on 42nd Street, sick-sweet molasses popcorn, gas main odors, the polluted Hudson and East rivers, hot pavement tar, rancid hamburgers, summer subways and whiskey exhaust from taverns.

But when I opened the door here this morning there was a fragrance of narcissus and lilac buds and fresh salt air, pines and firs and smoke from wood fires, wet dog and wet earth. And last night was one of those clear nights when one can almost smell the stars sparkling—quite a change from a glimpse of two stars through the blue smog of a Manhattan night.

There is some sort of bug in a cocoon now on the back porch. It was found on a flower in the garden, and we brought it in and set it under a glass custard cup to see what it would turn into. My husband is warning me it may be a swarm of praying mantises, but I cannot imagine that it contains more than one bug.

The longer I stay here, the sharper I hope I will be able to whet these deactivated senses of mine, for I know I still have in prospect the sight of deer crunching apples, rabbits burrowing under wild roses, bird tracks in the sand, moss in dank woods. And there will soon be roses to sniff at on Edgartown fences, and there are bell buoys to hark to.

I know I will miss Chinatown's pagoda telephone booths, French restaurants serving white beans and Madison Avenue on Saturdays, but it was only occasionally that I "turned on" to such things in the city. It will be good to be turned on always.

Dinosaurs
Shun
the
Vineyard

We have been fortunate and have rented the West Tisbury parsonage, an ambling eighteenth-century farmhouse. It has its own apple and pear trees, a brook and a field where the Congregational Church trustees permit a neighbor to graze a poor, tired old pony. At Alley's General Store, they tell me the pony has founder. I have asked what that is, and am told it is a painful hoof disease. The pony is understandably snappish if we go too close to the fence, and some evenings he seems to grow quite mad and race from one end of the field to the other, neighing fiercely and snapping his head to and fro. But it is pleasant, all the same, to look out a window and see a horse grazing in a field—when one is accustomed to looking down thirteen stories onto a red light and beeping taxicabs and sacks of garbage and rusted springs set out for the city refuse collectors.

Across the road is one of the Island's few remaining working farms. The farmer has sheep and Black Angus and a horse or two (although he has no use for horses, they say) and grows potatoes. He is a jolly, cherubic man whose forebears settled across the road in the seventeenth century. He was sent off-Island to school—to Andover and Yale—but he came back as soon as his schooling was over. He has never wanted to live anywhere but the Island, he says, where he can scallop or ice-boat in winter, depending on his mood; hunt bluebills and deer in season; look after his cows and his sheep. He loves sheep, he insists, and when city folk ask the eternal question, "Aren't sheep dumb?" he snaps back proudly that they are no such thing—their mentality may be different from other animals', but their intelligence is certainly no less.

His wife is an intense woman who, these days, is masterminding the Island's Concerned Citizens organization in its fight against construction of a jet airport here.

The other night I awoke to hear hoofs beating on the front door, and when I opened it, one of the farm lambs gamboled in. He clattered about and pulled up the scatter rugs before we got him out again. Then he stood on the doorstep and looked mournful. Fog had sifted in over the moors with the coming of sundown; summer people had already begun to arrive and so there was traffic, and I worried about the lamb crossing the road alone. He is still young enough to be skittish and easily distracted, so we took him home. We sat for awhile and talked about farm animals and pets (we learned the lamb's name was Alfred Hitchcock as he curled up under the table in the kitchen in a possessive way) and I was reminded of a story of a Vineyard pet which my father had told me when I was a child. It is a story I have always enjoyed. I think he told it because I had asked for a dog and he didn't like dogs, so he suggested that I find myself a dinosaur instead. He said he had a great fondness for them, ever since he was a boy and had found a dinosaur egg under a bathhouse at the East Chop Beach Club.

He was on his way in from swimming one Sunday, he said, and there, big as life, was a dinosaur egg on the sand. He said he knew what it was right away because of the odd, swelled-out shape at the end where the dinosaur's neck was. He said it was almost as big as he was, and he was ten years old at the time. But he had managed to roll it, one way or another, up the road by the bluffs, taking great pains, of course, to see that it didn't crack on any of the stones it went over. A few people passed him, he said, on their way to the beach, carrying their striped beach umbrellas and beach chairs and wearing their rubber swimming shoes, and they smiled at him. But nobody said anything. They didn't know what it was he was rolling, he said.

He had gotten the egg home to the red-shingled cottage on Arlington Avenue at the top of the Downs, where he and his father and his mother and his grandfather and two grandmothers (belonging to different grandfathers, of course, he always explained) and a little sister spent their summers.

He had lugged the egg up the porch steps and into the drying room in back of the kitchen, and since his mother was out in the yard cranking Sunday ice cream, his father was reading the Sunday paper, his grandfather was reciting French proverbs to one grandmother (it was a very French family), and the other grandmother was knitting a sweater and was very deaf anyway, no one had seen the dinosaur egg but his little sister, and it hadn't been hard to keep her quiet.

He had explained to her, of course, what his find was. He

had whispered it to her as they sat in a laundry basket on a mound of fresh-smelling towels and sheets, and had told her that the dinosaur egg would have to be carefully guarded. It would probably have to be sat on from time to time to be hatched, too. Meanwhile, he suggested that it be hidden in the bottom of the laundry basket. Every hour or so, he said, it would be a good idea if she came out to the drying room and sat on it for fifteen minutes or so to help it hatch.

As the story went, the dinosaur egg stayed on in the laundry basket all day Sunday. It got sat on periodically and, all of a sudden, just at suppertime when everyone was sitting down to Edam cheese and lettuce salad, there was a noise in the drying room.

My father's father said, "What was that?"

My father's mother said it sounded like a roar.

One grandmother stopped eating lettuce.

The other grandmother stopped nibbling cheese.

My father's grandfather said he'd see what it was.

He grabbed the cane and started for the drying room.

My father's sister squeaked.

My father's grandfather pulled open the drying room door and there was the dinosaur, all hatched and shiny-eyed, sitting up in the laundry basket.

Of course, my father said, his grandfather had no idea what to do, any more than his father did, or one grandmother, or the other grandmother, or his sister. The only one with presence of mind in the situation was his mother.

She got up and looked in the laundry basket and said in a matter-of-fact German way, "Harrumph." (Everyone else in the family was French and that made a difference in presence-of-mindedness, I guess.)

She turned right to my father and asked where he'd got it. (About then the dinosaur climbed out of the laundry basket, came into the dining room, my father said, and looked appealingly at the Edam cheese.)

One of the grandmothers gave him a piece.

My father's father said you shouldn't feed animals at the table.

My father's grandfather still stood in the drying room with his cane over his shoulder like a javelin.

My father's father just sat.

So did the second grandmother.

My father's sister cried.

My father tried to pet the dinosaur. (He said, hatched, it was about the size of a six-year-old.) But he wasn't sure exactly where you petted dinosaurs. He thought maybe you just scratched at the ruffle that went down their backs, but he tried, and the dinosaur only kept looking at the cheese.

Anyway, my father's mother said the dinosaur had to go. My father's grandfather swore a French oath and said, "Yes, of course." My father's father said it was curious seeing a dinosaur face to face. He would have to write a book about it. Neither grandmother said anything.

My father told how he had found the dinosaur, unhatched, lying in the sand at the beach club, and had rolled it home. He told how he had put it in the drying room because the sun shone in and it would be warming and help it to hatch.

My father's mother looked frostily at the dinosaur, who was trying to put his front paws on the dining room table so he could get at a lettuce leaf. While he was doing it, his tail was swooshing back and forth perilously near her china closet.

My father said his mother put on her thoughtful expression. She had always reared her children by *Little Women,* he said. Whenever she put on her thoughtful expression in a family crisis he knew she was trying to figure out what Louisa May Alcott would have done. Finally she said the dinosaur could stay overnight, but he would have to be out in the morning.

After that, everyone retired to the porch to smoke pipes, swing in the hammock, recite more proverbs, listen to the crickets on the Downs and swat mosquitoes—except my father's mother, of course, who stayed in the kitchen to do the dishes and throw out the dinosaur shell.

My father's father said maybe she shouldn't do that—the Museum of Natural History in New York might be interested. But my father's mother said, "Nonsense." She wasn't going to have dinosaur shells cluttering up her kitchen, and she put it in the wastepaper basket.

Anyway, everyone else went out on the porch, including the dinosaur, after he had had enough Edam cheese and lettuce and a bowl of water my father's sister gave to him and showed him how to lap up.

The dinosaur curled up by the porch railing, very politely, flattened his ruffle and listened to the crickets, too. And when it got late and everyone went inside and sat down and began to read, the dinosaur went inside and was very careful not to slam the screen door with his tail. My father thought about offering him a book, but he said he guessed since he was a baby dinosaur he probably didn't know how to read yet.

That night the dinosaur slept under the dining room table when everyone else went to bed.

The next morning he woke up when the rest of the family did, and had a big dish of fresh blueberries for breakfast. Then my father's mother said it was time he left. She told my father to take the dinosaur with him when he went to the beach. She said she had no objection to pets, but with a dinosaur there was a certain growing problem. She said, anyway, dinosaurs were better off living outdoors.

My father asked, of course, how the dinosaur would keep

warm, and if the mosquitoes wouldn't annoy him at night. His mother said that since it was summer the weather was really no problem, and she thought he could take care of mosquitoes without any trouble. When it grew cold, she said, he'd surely find a house in the Camp Ground to move into.

My father's father kept saying things about taking him back to New York, to the Bronx Zoo or the Museum of Natural History for examination, but my father's mother just wasn't interested at all.

My father felt sad, of course, about just putting the dinosaur out like that. After all, he was quite a find. But wasn't much he could do about it as long as his mother had made up her mind that was the way things would have been handled in *Little Women*.

So they went down to the beach club together, and the dinosaur thought he was going to go for a swim, too, but my father said, no, he'd have to go back where he came from, and left him standing by the bathhouse steps.

My father said he dived into the water and didn't look back at the dinosaur for quite a while. When he did look up, all he could see was a swooshing tail disappearing around by the harbor. My father's sister said he'd probably gone right downtown to look for a winter cottage in Oak Bluffs.

Anyway, when I asked for a dog my father had said, no, but what he really would like was another dinosaur if I could find one. I remember that I looked by the bathhouses at the beach club six Sundays in a row, and I looked in all the windows of the cottages in the Camp Ground, but there weren't any dinosaurs.

I asked my mother where I could find one, and she said not to worry, perhaps there'd be some another summer. She said she'd heard there was a dinosaur shortage here on the Vineyard that year.

Travel
Abroad

I am just back from a trip abroad on which I found, oddly, that I am more under the spell of the Vineyard than I had thought. It seems too soon to have had so total a change of outlook, but ordinarily, when I have traveled, I have sought the excitement of cities. The bustle and neon lights of Piccadilly have been inviting; the cafés of Paris's Boul' Mich', and the tourists on Rome's Spanish Steps. But this time I found that I distinctly longed to be in smaller, quieter places. I wanted to be in mountain villages, listening to the hollow clang of cow bells and watching sun and shadow paths on golden fields of colza.

This spring, either colza has been more abundant than ever across Belgium and Germany and Switzerland, or my eyes have been turned more often toward the landscape than in the past, for I have never noticed colza before. At first, when it caught my eye, I thought the fields were filled with buttercups, and I smiled happily at the thought of so much purposeless prettiness. Then I realized that the yellow was too neatly laid out to be accidental, and I asked what it was that was growing so effulgently and was given the name colza, or rape seed, and told that oil comes from it and that cattle eat it. I wonder if the cattle find it is as delicious as it looks. It brightens pasture lands in such a lovely way and always makes them look as if sunlight had been entrapped in them.

Because of this curious longing for stillness and peace, even at those times when I was in cities, I chose to stay where I could feel, as much as possible, apart from them. In Paris, this was on a boat on the Seine, docked alongside the quay below the Pont Alexandre III where the winged horses of the bridge glittered in the early morning sun; the Eiffel Tower loomed mistily, and an old man fished at the quayside.

I munched an apple and watched long black coal barges pass, with their Canadian or American or Swiss or German pennants tossing, and their flowered curtains fluttering. Their crews waved and one sailor wished me a "Bon Appétit."

In Switzerland, I made certain I avoided Zurich. I paused briefly in Geneva and climbed to Lausanne's cathedral hilltop to look down over the rust-red rooftops to the lake and the mountains, but then I went on to the little walled town of Morat, where black ducks dived on the Morat lake and Saturday yachtsmen were pulling up sails for afternoon outings.

Although I was there on a gray afternoon, the whistling and singing of the sailors was not diminished by the cloudy skies or the whitecaps. Spray dashed over red and blue bows as sailboat after sailboat tacked across the lake toward hills checkered with the brown patches of grape vineyards.

I picnicked on a bench by the lakeside, eating crusty bread and Gruyère cheese. Bridal wreath tossed in the wind and miniature daisies poked their petals from the grass at my feet.

After lunch I ambled along the road above the lake, past sway-backed barns and yellow stucco farmhouses with balconies. From one, an orange bird in a cage chirped at me and his master nodded proudly.

Morat's ramparts are still intact for climbing, and four gray-clad Swiss soldiers and I climbed up them together to look below on twisted chimneys and tile roofs sloping so temptingly that had it not been for their scalelike structure one could have slid across the town on them. In gardens below, tulips and lettuces and cabbages were sprouting.

I went from Switzerland to Poland, and although my introduction to the latter was in Warsaw, I quickly fled to the smaller city of Cracow at the foot of the Carpathians. There on a limestone hilltop rises a brick-red and sand-gold sixteenth-century castle with copper dragons spouting from its roof, ivy twining and weeping willows sighing. I followed schoolchildren in mini-skirts and dungarees to it one after-noon, and sat with them in the courtyard while we waited for the castle to be opened for the day.

In its garden, workmen weeded from portable stools. Velvety-purple irises were everywhere, and yellow and purple pansies, and horse chestnut trees heavy with their white blooms. A great gray-headed, black-bodied bird flew down from a rampart in search of seeds. (Until this year, I have never noticed birds, but the Vineyard has made me alert to them.) Another plucked at the grass between the cobble-stones of the colonnaded courtyard where tournaments once were held. Little boys whistled to attract pigeons.

Later, I went to the Cracow marketplace to be among the flowers and the flower sellers. There were green pails full of pansies and roses and lilacs, and their sellers, in long skirts, padded vests and kerchiefs as protection against the cold, crocheted and chatted, and drank tea from red tin cups.

But Cracow, its castle gardens and its flower sellers notwithstanding, is city not country, and my yearning still was for the countryside, so I took a trip outside the city to watch the sun set one afternoon behind the jutting white rocks of Ojcow, fifteen miles away. Enroute, I passed through green, green fields, and by thatched-roofed cottages of stucco "blue like the sky," Polish companions told me. Birch trees wavered in the wind. Elderly women and small girls herded brown and white cows on the hillsides.

There were other stops on my trip—in Belgian forests, Germany's Schwäbische Alps, among the cabbage patches outside Stuttgart. I ate white asparagus and sun-smoked ham in rustic restaurants, and picked apple blossoms with a smiling child with braids.

I am glad to have been traveling, for it always refreshes one's thoughts, but it is good to be back, too. For here, there is no need to search for fields and streams and sailboats and pine woods. For a little while yet, they are still on the Vineyard almost everywhere.

Pixie Cups
and Spats
and
Pudding
Stones

Since I have been on the Vineyard, my vocabulary has increased by leaps and bounds. A week or so ago I was told to go out the Lobsterville Road and watch the seagulls pip.

"Peep?" I said.

"Pip," I was firmly told. Of course, apologetically, I asked what pipping was.

With a sigh that distinctly suggested that I should be better informed, I was told then that baby seagulls (and most birds) rotate 360 degrees to get out of their shells, then peck with their egg tooth on the egg cap until the shell breaks. This constitutes pipping.

"Egg tooth?" I said. "Do birds have teeth?"

Three months ago, of course, I would have been far too

sophisticated to ask such a silly question. But that was before I learned that robins "listen" to worms underground and then swoop down to pull them out.

Yes indeed, many birds have teeth, I was told. Egg teeth are most prominent, however, in waterfowl, pheasants, quail and chicken-like birds. An egg tooth is a knobby tip on the end of a bird's bill that it loses about two days after hatching. And the egg cap (of which I had never heard either) is the large, rounded end of the shell where the baby bird elects to break his way out.

All this bird talk took place by the West Tisbury Mill Pond, and the swans were gliding up and down in their usual, graceful, gracious way.

"What an attractive pen," my companion said.

"Where?" I asked, ruffling searchingly in the grass with my big toe.

"Pen," my companion said a trifle querulously. "Pen, you know, female swan."

And so I have been working to fatten my vocabulary. I now know, for example, that male swans are cobs. In my quest for more such information I have been to see Gus Ben David, the director of the Felix Neck Wildlife Sanctuary. I have explained to him that too many Island conversations are above my head, and have asked his aid. I told him about one such conversation that I had with the director of the state lobster hatchery.

We were talking about oysters when he suddenly said, "The spat sets on the cultch."

"Beg pardon," I said.

He repeated, "The spat sets on the cultch."

There was no pretending I knew anything about that one. I looked ashamed and sought an explanation.

When an oyster is ready to spawn, I was told, it is called a spat, and, at that time, oystermen put down a bed of scallop and oyster shells for it to attach itself to. The bed is the cultch.

At the lobster hatchery, I also learned that whales have tusks (not teeth, like birds) and big male bass are bulls.

I have asked Mr. Ben David what other curious words and phrases I am likely to be mystified by here.

He wanted to know if I knew that baby skunks were kittens and that raccoons purred. He also asked if I knew that sea robins walked and penguins flew under water, and he told me that most sea birds were colonials. (Of course, this has led me to visions of pompous penguins and stuffy auklets in pith helmets and walking shorts.)

Mr. Ben David has also warned me that three or four crows meeting together on my field are not a flock or a bunch but a murder. As for the pheasants that spruce up by the fence across the road, together they form a bouquet.

I have learned that although hovercraft may hover, the only birds that do are sparrow hawks and rough-legged and red-tailed hawks. Hovering, it seems, is a very difficult gyration that involves facing into the wind and remaining in one spot with the constant flapping of wings and the tail tilting downwards. Hawks, and hawks alone, are constructed to assume such a pose.

Mrs. John A. Gillespie, a bird watcher and bird bander for decades, has informed me that female sandpipers are reeves and males are ruffs. And she asked me the other day if I knew what British soldiers and pixie cups were. I ventured that British soldiers must be cardinals (thinking of the red coats, of course). She looked offended and said both British soldiers and pixie cups are lichens that grow everywhere in up-Island pastures.

I have learned on a beach walk with another naturalist that

a shore covered with shingle is covered with flat stones and that bluebill ducks bobbing in any number form a raft.

From Norman G. Benson, who retired five years ago after 57 years as a trap fisherman, I learned about pudding stones (a mass of little stones that somehow have all come together to form one big stone) and that chummies and mummy chugs are minnows. He also told me about the three incarnations of a sea trout—how they used to be weakfish but they failed to sell with such an unappetizing name, so they were called squeteague, an Algonquin word that means "they make glue." At last, he said, the lowly weakfish has climbed the social ladder to become sea trout, a most marketable fish.

For years I have wondered what those horny, dry black cases are that one finds on beaches. I asked an Island child about them the other day as we combed South Shore together for driftwood. "They're sea purses, of course," he said, and went on to explain that they are the egg cases of skates and certain kinds of sharks.

I have learned that an unkind name for a porpoise is a sea hog and that, when jellyfish bob together offshore and make me nervous about tangling with their tentacles, they are grouped together in a smack.

Since I have been a country dweller for only a month and a half, I think I have done remarkably well. By next spring, surely, my scrabble game will be unbeatable!

Sir Edward Elgar's Daughter Reminisces

From day to day on the Vineyard, one never knows whom one will meet. Last Saturday I was told, for example, that the daughter of the late Sir Edward William Elgar, composer of the familiar graduation march, *Pomp and Circumstance,* was on the Island, and I was asked to stop by for a visit.

She is staying in Menemsha at the Beach Plum Inn, down a dirt road in a cottage among the beach plums and huckleberry bushes. It is an out-of-the-way place where rabbits hop about boldly and catbirds call.

Mrs. Carice Elgar Blake of Bristol, England, has just ended an exhausting month-long fund-raising tour of the United States and Bermuda, and wouldn't, she says, "have missed the Island for anything."

She has been enjoying the absence of billboards, which she found virtually everywhere else in the country, watching Menemsha fishermen bring in their catches in their fat trawlers, and simply strolling about in the towns, which remind her of England.

We talked on the porch of her little cottage and watched the birds and the animals in the foliage. ("I don't believe we have catbirds in England at all—and beach plums, we hadn't a clue about those!") With her is a friend, Miss H. Sybil Russell.

The up-Island moors, too, she said, remind her of England, with their gray-blueness and rocks scattered here and there, an occasional thistle and the sea always at hand. Mrs. Blake reminisced about her father and told of her efforts to raise $50,000 in this country to maintain, in perpetuity, the Midlands cottage where he was born. For a number of years now, the cottage, which is in Broadheath, has been a museum, established by the city of Worcester near which it lies, but it needs continuing care.

"It's really a perfectly ordinary brick cottage," Mrs. Blake said. "It has a lovely garden, but the country round is getting rather built over, wouldn't you say?" she asked her companion.

"Oh, I'd still say it's country," Miss Russell, a former Women's Auxiliary Air Force officer, replied. "And in any case, it's a house filled with all sorts of interesting things. All of Sir Edward's manuscripts are there, and books, and his Order of Merit and various degrees, including one from Yale.

"And there's an immense correspondence with Bernard Shaw," added Mrs. Blake. "They were very great friends. They used to meet and have long talks, and there are letters from W.B. Yeats and George Moore and Paderewski and Chaliapin."

"When he was in London, living in Hampstead," Miss Russell said, "Sir Edward was considered one of the most literary of people. He knew Shakespeare inside out, and he was very fond of Thomas Gray and Ben Jonson. He was a tremendous scholar, wasn't he?"

"Indeed he was," his daughter replied. "It's a pity that here in this country you don't know more about him. All he's known for at all here seems to be P. and C., and a great many people here have told us even though they'd had the march for every graduation, they didn't know who wrote it."

"P. and C.?" I asked.

"Well, you can't say *Pomp and Circumstance* all the time, can you? Certainly not when you talk about it as much as we do," Mrs. Blake said. "I suppose you knew there were five P. and C.'s?"

I admitted I didn't, and added that I hadn't the faintest idea what the title came from.

"Why, it's a Shakespearian quotation," Mrs. Blake said. "I have a feeling it's from *Othello* but I'm not certain."

"Probably," said Miss Russell, popping up efficiently to get a wrap for Mrs. Blake who had shivered slightly.

"It's intended, anyway, to give the idea of pageantry," Mrs. Blake explained.

She is a pretty, white-haired woman, inclined toward rose-hued clothing that complements her blue-green eyes and pink cheeks.

"As I said," she continued, "there are five P. and C.'s—P. and C.1-2-3-4-5, we call them. Each one has an entirely different tune. The one that you know has the words 'Land of Hope and Glory' to be sung to it. They were composed by A.C. Benson, a scholar at Cambridge, and my father liked the words and took them. That version, for us, is rather a national hymn. 'Land of hope and glory, mother of the free.'

other war works included *For the Fallen, To Women,* and *With Proud Thanksgiving.* Inspired by John Cardinal Newman's poem, *The Dream of Gerontius,* Sir Edward wrote an oratorio of the same name that is usually considered his masterpiece. It is concerned with the death of Everyman, with his going on to another world and his being cared for there by a guardian angel.

"There is one brief glimpse of the Almighty, and the music is simply shattering," said Miss Russell. "What does 'Gerontius' mean? Well, it's the name of the hero. It's from the Greek—geron—for old man."

"I wish I had gone to the first performance of *Gerontius,* but I couldn't because I was barely ten," Mrs. Blake said sorrowfully.

"After that, there was an oratorio called *The Apostles*—the story of the Crucifixion. It was commissioned for the Birmingham Festival, which was very important. And then there was *The Kingdom* in 1906. That's after *The Ascension.* It has to do with the choosing of the Apostle to replace Judas."

"Really, he did some remarkable things," said Miss Russell, "that's why we're so eager about our project. If you know anyone who would like to contribute, please ask them to write to Elgar's Birthplace, Broadheath, Worcestershire. Finally, in the reign of Edward VII he became Master of the King's Music."

"Now I think I'd better put that right," corrected Mrs. Blake, but not unkindly. "It was in the time of George V, but he was a great friend of Edward VII. My mother made a point of making herself known to the people who mattered and was wonderful for him."

"Tell about your name," said Miss Russell.

"Oh—my name. Well, before my father and mother were

married, he wrote a piece called *Salut d'Amour.* He wanted to dedicate it to my mother, but he didn't want anyone to know it. Her name was Caroline Alice, so he took the 'Car' from Caroline and the 'ice' from Alice and dedicated it to Carice. But whoever had such a name! Carice Elgar Blake! I kept the Elgar after I was married because so many people had known my father.

Mrs. Blake stopped, captivated by the sight of a sparrow which, she said, was nothing at all like a genuine English sparrow. She is particularly fond of life in the country because from the time of her marriage until her husband's death in 1939, she lived in the country, where he raised sheep and cattle.

"That, I expect, is why I've enjoyed Martha's Vineyard so," she said.

Summer Morning

Summer came last month and I walked out along the Lambert's Cove Road early one morning to meet it. It was shortly before seven when I set out, awakened by a robin in the maple outside my window. It was heralding the day with such delight that only the laziest of slugabeds would have failed to stir.

Roadsides and meadows are sprinkled now with daisies and dandelions. The fragrance of multiflora rose clusters was in the air. A velvet bumblebee was having a honeysuckle breakfast on a moss-backed wall, and a bobwhite was calling. I was glad to be out before the rest of the world was stirring.

There are those, I know, who claim that summer nights are more captivating than summer days. Just after sundown, after all, there are whippoorwills calling in Indian Hill woods. Fireflies flash and crickets chirp. Frogs seem to pluck violin strings and the songs of the pinkletinks replace bird songs. On a clear night, the stars invite identification. I have always been fascinated by the stories of the stars—the Great and Little Bears, victims of a jealous Juno; Orion with his sword and club; the pretty Pleiades whom he pursued. But I am always cross when I cannot fit the stars into these intriguing shapes. Even the Big and Little Dippers escape me, so if I walk on summer evenings, I am inclined to favor fog and mist that cloud the stars, diffuse light, make trees and houses loom and put a mystery in the air that I have no urge to comprehend.

Perhaps it is because of this that I am a morning walker. I know that if I wish to hear all the birds in the woods, I should be up before dawn, but simply being out early enough to find the day still fresh and untouched is satisfying.

There was a rabbit hurrying home sheepishly after a night's carousing—or at least it seemed to me that there was something sheepish about his hesitation when he saw me. He looked distinctly caught-in-the-act; he waited till I had passed and then hopped over a rock and into the underbrush.

Peering down where he had hopped, I found a brook tumbling, banked with dew-damp brown leaves. Green ferns were sprouting, and I wondered if, in season, watercress might grow there, for it reminded me of a New Hampshire brook where I used to gather that crisp green delicacy.

I followed a path up a hillside blue-gray with furze into a clearing. I was just speculating on the site's possibilities as a picnic spot when the gnats came in droves, and I fled to the road, batting them away from my hair where they had become entangled.

It was a pity because, from all other standpoints, it was

such a perfect hill for laying out a blanket on a sunny day, reading a book, eating a juicy tomato and munching ham sandwiches with pickles.

By then I was beginning to be hungry, for my eye was next attracted to a house with a screened-in porch where, I thought, cornflakes and fresh peaches would taste particularly delicious.

A bicyclist appeared in the distance. As he grew closer, we looked at each other stony-faced, for each, I'm sure, was intruding where the other thought he was alone—and wished to be. But it was much too cheerful a day to be possessive and ugly-tempered. We seemed to have the same thought simultaneously, and nodded and called "hi"—not nearly so pretty a greeting as an Austrian "Greet God," but there is a certain hearty friendliness to it all the same.

When the bicyclist had gone, I began wildflower gathering—in a somewhat desultory way, but that is appropriate, I think, to the picking of wildflowers. Each should lead you to another till you have strayed far from your starting place, as each beach plum bush leads the plum picker to a new dune with a new view of beach grass and Sound.

A pink-lavender clover burr was what I first picked. And, of course, I was soon tempted to search for four-leaf clovers. But the first of the morning's wheezing cars interrupted the clover hunt. I climbed higher on the road bank after a viburnum (arrow-wood it is also called, I'm told, for its strong wood made the best arrows).

As I looked across the road, a pond was sparkling invitingly. A fish or insect was making a mosaic of circles in the water, so I went off to investigate. I climbed the fence I came to with a certain amount of trepidation, for a "No Trespassing" sign in the driveway informed me that I was on the Dukes County sheriff's land.

Dime-sized, almond-shaped creatures were darting about just below the surface of the water, and I am told that they were probably tadpoles. I toyed with trying to catch one, but then I heard voices and crockery and table-setting sounds from the sheriff's house above the pond. A screen door opened and shut, and, like the sheepish rabbit, I hurried back to the main road, reaching it just as the sheriff's black sedan nosed out of the driveway.

It is interesting to me how curiously those who drive by in cars regard a walker who is simply walking, not hitchhiking. Heads are invariably craned; the car slows down for a better look at such a strange phenomenon. The walker feels a certain sense of guilt. He wonders if he is really odd to be enjoying walking and seeing sights so much better seen on foot than through the streaky glass of a car window. From an automobile, after all, one misses bumblebees and humming-birds and huckleberry blossoms hugging the ground. All the small sights and sounds and subtler smells of the earth and flowers are summer attractions the car rider cannot know.

I walked as far as the Lambert's Cove Cemetery, where a miniature flag was snapping smartly on a veteran's grave. A swallow was swooping over the hummocks, and the avenue of trees at the hilltop was swaying.

Then I started back. Half a dozen cars had passed by then—scarcely traffic—but too much activity to allow much contemplation.

By the time I reached Cottle's Lumberyard, workmen were already hammering and sawing. The cleaner's delivery truck was making its rounds. A milk truck drove by.

I added a blossom that looked to me like phlox gone wild (the wildflower book inelegantly calls it bladder campion) to my bouquet, some daisies, something yellow I could not identify and a bit of that rough-stalked meadow grass they call blue grass, and then I headed home. There, to cap the morning, a quail was courting—whistling and prancing round his intended—and a white butterfly was darting over the pink pasture roses.

Moon
Legends

The moon is in a dark phase now, and I find that I miss it. Its absence has been making me recall moonflooded nights by the East Chop lighthouse when I was a child; nights when the moon rode wave crests at South Beach; and times when its reflection quivered on inland Island waters—still ponds that are almost, but not quite, still.

At the ponds, when the moon is full, there always seem to be hefty frog voices.

And sometimes on a moonlit night, I have seen rabbits chasing each other in wild rose patches, and Queen Anne's lace looking like Belgian lace laid out to dry in a field.

On such nights, sounds seem to come clearer and scents to grow more fragrant. It is probably only imagination that makes these things seem so, but a night when the moon is shining is a particularly tempting one for a woodland walk, crunching a leaf of yarrow to heighten its spiciness, or a needle of spruce for its balm. There is no better time, either, to seek out the beetlebung or a gnarled cedar stretched against the sky. In moonglow, there can be much melancholy.

It is on moonlit nights, of course, that Island ghosts are abroad, the old-timers say. A woman in a long gown was walking across the Gay Head flats last spring, lifting her skirts above the grass, but never stopping anywhere—only endlessly walking. And many years ago, the disembodied head of a beautiful, long-haired girl was seen hovering in the moonlight that streamed in through the windows of a Gay Head bedroom. The moon at Gay Head lights up all the fields like daybreak, they say. "Why, you can pick up a pin in the Gay Head moonlight," I've been told.

Legends and superstitions about the moon abound here as they do everywhere. A new moon, for example, should first be glimpsed over one's right shoulder—a superstition that has always caused me trouble because it means, before setting out on a new moon night, one must be sure where the moon will be. Sometimes I have even gone out a door backwards to be in an advantageous position.

The Indians say that if their forebears could hang their powder horns on a quarter moon, they believed dry days would lie ahead—that is, if the moon was almost straight across the sky. When a quarter moon is tipped, water can spill out. Similarly, old Island farmers maintain that if a bucket will not hang on the prongs of a quarter moon, then it is a wet moon and a poor time to cut hay.

And there is a Gay Head story that weaning children in a certain phase of the moon will keep them from sucking their thumbs, except that it has been forgotten which phase is the appropriate one. There is also a saying that an overdue mother-to-be will be certain to have her child at the first full moon.

And another saying is that women should only cut their hair when the moon is full. This assures that their locks will grow lustrous and thick.

Cyril Norton always pulls a boat out of the water for painting when the moon is full—although it is a practical, rather than a superstitious matter. "It's just common sense to pull a boat out on a high tide," he explained to me the other day. "You copper paint her on one side. Then when the tide comes in again, you roll her over and paint her on the other side."

And at full moon, particularly in the spring when the tide is strong, fishermen catch the most cod and fluke. Stripers and bluefish and mackerel, they say, come in greatest numbers at a full moon, for the riptides are the strongest then and ball up a rod-and-reel fisherman's bait, making it seem larger and more succulent to the fish he is after.

Conversely, though, swordfish usually come up to fin only at slack tide when there is a quarter moon.

As for lobsters, pots in deep water should be pulled when the tide is weak and the buoys show. When the tide is running high, the buoys are swept underwater.

And there are, of course, birds that seem to be affected by the moon. The woodcock sings later in the evening under a full moon, and the yellow-breasted chat and the cuckoo seem to sing particularly madly then.

There once were men on the Island, as there were elsewhere, who planted their crops according to the phases of the moon—and there still is one who keeps such information in the back of his mind. Leafy vegetables—asparagus, broccoli, cabbage, celery, parsley and spinach—are best planted in the first quarter of the moon. Beans, eggplant, melons, peas and other viney annuals do best when planted in the moon's second quarter. Lawns should be mowed in the first and second quarters to increase growth and in the third and fourth quarters to decrease growth.

Fence posts are best set out when the moon is old. They are less likely, then, to come out.

And there are cooks, too, who still bake by the moon here. One West Tisbury baker tells me that it is certain that bread rises higher and is lighter when the moon is increasing.

But here on the Island there were once mooncussers, too, who detested the light of the moon. Most of them were in Chilmark where they preyed on grounded vessels a hundred or more years ago. The light of the moon interfered with their carrying off as much loot as they would have liked before insurance men came to evaluate a wreck.

As I have thought of the Vineyard and the moon, I have gone looking for moon shells with circular collars and those highly polished round white stones that one calls moon-stones, even though they are not, of course, the semi-precious kind. And I have also recalled that curiously squashed glassy disc that was found at Gay Head ten years ago, and that some identified as tektite—a piece of moon splashed out, one scientist maintained, when a meteorite struck the moon.

The moon on an island, like the moon in the mountains, seems so very close.

The Lobster Hunt

Got your lobster pot and a boat?" asked the lobsterman. "Got a fifty-pound cement block and twenty-five fathoms of warp?"

This morning I peered around the door of Donald Poole's lobstering shack at Menemsha and asked how I could become a weekend lobsterman.

"Why, you're too small to be a lobsterman," Captain Poole said. "Worse than that. You're a woman."

I am five feet, six inches tall and weigh 115 pounds. I asked why that was not big enough to hunt lobsters.

Captain Poole eyed me with that uncomprehending look reserved for city folk who insist on stewing their own rose hip jam, picking wild blackberries in bramble patches and making elderberry wine.

"What do you want to catch lobsters for?" he asked. "Go to my son's fish market and buy them."

That was exactly what I no longer wanted to do. So often when swimming, I have tangled with lobster buoys a few yards offshore and dreamed of broiled, breadcrumb-stuffed, home-caught lobsters. The idea of do-it-yourself lobsters is appealing. Also, I find the fish market price for a lobster drearily high. When I awoke this morning I began wondering why I could not go lobstering myself and set off to Menemsha after the necessary accessories. Captain Poole has been a lobsterman for close to half a century. His shack seemed the right place to stop to learn what I might need.

"Got a license?" he asked, first crack out of the box. "That'll cost you $10 right there."

I said I wanted to find out, first, how to hunt lobsters.

"Buy a pot," he advised. "I favor half-round tops myself. But a friend of mine comes from down east way and up there they use square pots. And you can't catch a round-topped lobster in a square-topped pot." The lobster, he went on to explain, is a persnickity creature. Each lobstering port develops the type of pot that catches neighborhood lobsters best.

"Where can I buy a pot?"

"Most pots will cost you $10, but a fellow here built some that you could probably have for around $5."

"Good," I said. "Round pots?"

"Square pots."

"Can you catch lobsters in them?"

"Nope, not around here, but they'd do for you, I expect."

We went outside his shack and along the dock toward a mound of empty, sun-bleached, wooden-slatted lobster pots. Lobster pots resemble enlarged cat-carrying cases. I studied them with newly kindled professional interest.

"You've got two parts to a lobster pot," said my preceptor. "There's the kitchen and the parlor. Here's how it works."

The lobster enters the pot through a string funnel, he explained, and finds itself in the first compartment, the kitchen. Behind this is a second string funnel leading to the second compartment, the parlor. The bait hangs over the parlor door. The lobster nibbles at the bait and ends up in a befuddled state going through the second funnel into the parlor.

Occasionally, a lobster gets out of a pot by making a beeline through the front funnel, provided it keeps its claws in close and swims calmly. However, this probably does not happen often.

"What should I use for bait?" I inquired.

"Well," he said, "if you salt your bait, you need a fifty-pound cement block and an oak barrel. Then you need some swordfish trimmings and some swordfish backbones and some sea robins, if you have them, and a bit of brine. You put it all together, put the block on top and let it set till it stinks. The bait's no good until it'll kill a fly dead when he flies by."

He next showed me a lobster gauge which resembles a beer can opener. This is to measure the lobster from its eye socket to the end of its carapace.

"That's where the tail hitches on," Captain Poole explained before I could ask.

To be of legal size in Massachusetts, it seems, a lobster must measure at least three and three-sixteenths inches from the eye socket to the end of the carapace.

Captain Poole asked me if I could row. He wanted to know if I understood that you pulled your pots from the bottom every day and used a cement block to anchor them. He explained about the twenty-five fathoms of warp—the line that attaches the buoy to the trap. He added that, in case I did not know, there are six feet to a fathom.

He asked if I really thought I was strong enough to pull up 150 feet of line with a fifty-pound waterlogged pot at the end.

"And a pound and a half for the lobster," I said.

The best place to drop pots at this time of year is about a hundred feet offshore, according to Captain Poole. Lobsters have changed their ways, he also observed, and I should stay away from rocky ledges. Vineyard lobsters do not frequent them anymore. I should lobster hunt on the mud, instead.

Still not entirely deterred, I drove to the State Lobster Hatchery in Oak Bluffs to apply for a lobster- and crab-hunting license. Besides the usual data about name, age, address, height and weight, I was asked the color scheme of the buoys that would mark my pots.

I learned that my buoys must have different markings from any others in whatever port I choose to lobster from. Since I am not yet regarded as a year-round resident, a non-resident's license is what I had to apply for. It will allow me to lobster in June, July, August and September, and I had to agree to keep a record of my catch and file a report.

John Hughes, the marine biologist at the hatchery, told me that all the lobsters he knew were fussy eaters and now preferred fresh bait to salt. He suggested a pound of fluke scraps, placed in a loosely knit burlap bag tied with rubber tubing from an old inner tube. He said I could get the burlap at a bait or boating goods store and the inner tube at any old dump.

He also told me I should have a supply of empty, corked champagne or whiskey bottles to help the buoys to float. I would also need a "live car," another trap-like affair in which one stores lobsters until eating time, and a dock or mooring to attach it to.

Finally, Mr. Hughes said, there really would be no point in putting down fewer than twelve pots, in which case I might catch twenty-five lobsters a week if the lobstering were good. Correspondingly, if it were poor and I had only one pot, I suppose I might not catch any lobsters at all.

Twelve pots at $10 apiece are $120; 1,800 feet of warp at five cents a foot is $90; a skiff comes to $150; a live car, like the license, is $10; and the buoys cost from $1.50 to $3 each. The cement blocks come with the pots.

I ought to be able to find an old barrel in the West Tisbury dump, borrow a gauge, and, since there is no premium on swordfish backbones and limp skate, as far as I know, I expect I could get the bait free. All the same, I estimate a $398 minimum outlay for a twelve-pot lobster hunt. Or, if I control my appetite, and go in for only one-pot lobstering, I might manage for a little less than $200. Lobsters at the fish market? They're running $1 to $1.50 a pound. Now that I have second thoughts on the matter, that really isn't expensive at all.

Storm
and
Calm

This week I have been watching storm and sun and trying to choose between the two. Which do I like better? Why? I begin to think I have put an unanswerable pair of questions to myself. When the northeast wind blew Tuesday, and the sea thrashed and beach grasses were pulled low to the sand—the way a cat's ears are when it goes into narrow places—I was sure that I preferred storm wildness to the tranquility of a sunny day. But when morning came, and the sky was a Delft blue dusted with handfuls of clouds, and still, damp, drift roads were dappled with light, and the shadows of cornstalks danced on an Indian Hill barn, I was not so sure any longer.

There had been exhilaration in the tempest of the night

before, but in the calm of the fresh-washed morning, I was
mesmerized. The fragrance of the woodland evoked so many
recollections of other woodlands where sun had sparkled,
dreams had been dreamed, hopes realized and laughter
sounded.

I remembered a picnic in Germany's Black Forest at a time
when I still believed that gnomes and witches and wolves
were its principal inhabitants, and when, to my surprise, I
found that much of it is hardly suitable as a witch habitat at
all, for witches thrive on spotted toadstools and in dark
places, and I was among tall, graceful pines beside a silvery
brook.

And walking once in a Cornish wood, I stopped by the
roadside to write down my dreams of what I hoped would
one day be, while a curious bluejay watched me. (Bluejays, I
think, are always curious—their eyes are never anything but
bright; their heads are invariably cocked. I have never seen a
bluejay that was not alert.)

There was a bluejay watching me at Indian Hill Wednesday. I saw him when I stopped to gather acorn cups to make
doll goblets.

The dust that passersby and automobiles disperse had been
washed off all the plants along the road. The sea-green lichen
on the trees that the old legends say were bent to make an
Indian trail were the color of the copper roofs of Copenhagen.

Even if it seems I wished I were in all these places—
Cornwall, Copenhagen, the Black Forest—rather than on the
Indian Hill Road, it was not so at all. Long before I had ever
heard of them, when I was a child summering here, I walked
at Indian Hill, explored overgrown paths, picked high-bush
blueberries for the pies my grandmother made, and silver-
gray bayberries I thought I could cook till they became

candlewax, so all this is mine the way no distant land can ever be.

Rain beads were still glistening on the blades of grass beside the road when I went out Wednesday. They made the blades like diamond-studded brooches. A milkweed plant had been toppled by the wind and I squeezed some of the sticky milk from one of its firm fat pods for no particular reason except, I suppose, that it was there and I was curious about the texture of the pod.

I had squeezed milkweed pods before, but always playfully, never thinking about fuzzy textures.

At Arrowhead Farm, a woman picking flowers in the field was, clearly, in the same sort of reverie that I was, for she stopped happily every now and then to smell each blossom.

Turning back toward Christiantown, where, they say, the white men who came to the Vineyard from England early preached to the Indians, a brown oak leaf and green fern carpet invited me deeper into the woods. The rain had softened the leaves to make walking quiet. The only sounds were a crow cawing now and then, and that woodland buzzing noise that I think must be crickets.

I passed a house still redolent of a wood fire—I assumed of the night before—for Tuesday's pelting rain and buffeting wind was surely the kind that called for a fireplace blaze. It took me back to the Edgartown-Oak Bluffs road along the Sound, where I had been during the northeaster, and where a lone white wild rose had seemed to be struggling to free itself from its wind-beaten bush. It looked as if it wished to fly away from its stem and soar with the wind, across the road to where a seagull wheeled over Sengekontacket Pond and a white rowboat was foundering.

The bayberry had been huddled against the dunes. The grape leaves had turned their pale undersides to the wind, as if to protect the handsomer, deep green side that ordinarily shows. Seaweed tendrils, like drowned hair, were strewn on the beach.

When the sea rages, it seems so unfathomable and so much more mysterious than on calm days. There are so many more stories in its gray, churned depths and lashing waves. Beach pilings look so lonely in a storm. The white trim on a seaside house seems so much whiter when the weathered shingles are melted into the platinum gray of sky and green of sea.

The waves on Tuesday had been scaling the Oak Bluffs sea wall when I reached there and had gotten out of my car to stand a moment or two and be pelted angrily by the spray for my intrusion. At the harbor, slicker-clad men were bailing their boats. No one sat on the porch of Oak Bluffs' Victorian Camp Ground cottages, and I noticed how the happy salmon-pink of sunlit days looked faded and dreary in the rain, and the porches seemed to be sagging. One should be inside, never outside, a summer house when the wind and rain are in a fury. That is a time for cocoa and popping popcorn and playing solitaire. Summer cottage porches are meant for sunny days.

When I was a child, I spent my summers in a big Victorian house on East Chop, and in northeasters, we always had a fire in the stone fireplace and sprinkled salt on it to make the flames change color. We always made sure we had the sort of fire we would want to return to after a storm watch, or a daring swim in the surf.

Anyway, I am still in my quandary—which is a quandary of life, too, of course. Which is to be preferred, excitement or tranquility?

Disenchanted Journey

A few days ago, I went beachcombing on the Katama shore. The last time I was beachcombing there it was June and I followed the tracks of shore birds, watched sandpipers strutting, and collected a few chunks of cork and some sweet-smelling cedar posts washed in from somewhere. I found a piece of sea glass, muted a soft green by the winter-long action of sand and salt. I walked for an hour, I expect, and watched the waves and listened to the wind. Now and again, a fellow beachcomber passed and we nodded and smiled, though we eyed each other's treasures covetously.

This week, I beachcombed again in the same place. I started where Herring Creek crosses Katama Road, meandered along the creek for a while and then walked the beach.

The minnows were swimming in the creek, darting in and out among the water weeds. The bayberry smelled pungent, and the beach roses were plump with Chinese red hips that, eaten out of hand, provide an unusual taste treat.

Sea gulls circled overhead in the late afternoon, seeking, like me, the trophies of the shore. And for them, it seemed, there were many after a day of picnicking. More to the minnows' liking, however, than to either the sea gulls' or mine was my first midsummer beachcombing find. It was a white toothpaste tube curled at the bottom of Herring Creek. Soon, in the blooming yarrow, I made my other discoveries.

Let me explain that what I was seeking was whatever abounded on the beach at this time of year—Russian fish barrels, should I happen upon them; bottles containing messages; driftwood; polished stones—or man-made litter and garbage, if that was what was in profusion instead.

In the yarrow, it was a glistening aqua and silver potato chip bag that caught my eye. Hard by, a green and white spearmint chewing gum wrapper was sifting its way out of the sand. Near a slate-gray sea gull feather, paper plates were blowing in the beach grass, and a yellowed Aug. 3 *Boston Sunday Globe* was advertising an $8.95 scarf dress.

Vying for attention with the blue-purple bells of wild indigo was crumpled wax paper. Nestled in a clump of bright red wild cranberries was a brown beer bottle and a bill from the Harborside Inn, situated, said the letterhead, "on the storybook island of Martha's Vineyard." A ferry schedule, pale blue styrofoam from a beach cooler, a *Parade* magazine article on the "unspoiled beauty of Tahiti," and two chartreuse plastic spoons completed my Herring Creek finds.

At the parking lot itself, a Kodak Limited, London, film wrapper suggested that it is not Americans alone who litter. A beer can carrier of plastic was twisted in the huckleberry bushes. A matchbook cover told me that Martha's Vineyard was New England's finest resort, and I wondered as I picked it up—along with a hank of salmon-colored yarn, a smashed Coca Cola can and more blue styrofoam—how much longer the matchbook characterization would hold true with such litterbugs on the rampage.

Once I was on the beach itself, there was an even choicer collection of items to choose from. The first dune I reached was festooned with flowered yellow toilet paper and an interesting illustrated article on sex. A red and orange Frito package was blowing out of the beach peas. Some people, clearly, do try to keep the shores clean, for the Edgartown highway department's green barrel was filled to overflowing. A stack of cans and bottles and sticks of wood had been placed beside it by others eager to keep the shorefront litter-free. But a beach frequenter whom I passed told me that the barrel had not been emptied in more than a week.

As I continued my saunter across the sands, a pile of forty-six beer cans bore witness to a jolly party. Cheese spread in a plastic container and pastry in a plastic bag apparently had topped off that repast. The rustiness of the can midden suggested that it had lain there for at least a month.

Sand castles and children in the waves captured my fancy, and I took off my own shoes and walked along where the sands are golden and cool and damp. There, in the curly pink Irish moss, lay a box that once had held licorice candy.

I passed a guitarist strumming on his back in the sand, watching white clouds sweep by across the blue sky. A prescription from Brodsky's Pharmacy in Providence and a discarded green bottle that once had held suntan lotion lay near the dreamy guitarist's head.

There was a brown bottle decorated with a frosty Alpine

peak labeled "made in Switzerland" and I was horrified to think a Swiss might have littered, for I have always thought them the most litter-conscious people in the world, but the label further said "distributed in Rochester, N.Y." What a pity, I sighed to myself, that Island visitors—or Islanders, whoever the guilty ones may be—fail to treasure and protect the Vineyard dunes as Swiss do their soaring mountains, sparkling streams, gleaming glaciers and larch woods.

A sunning couple whom I passed, and to whom I explained my quest, directed me to a pile of rubble in the grass over a dune. This time there were whiskey half pints in paper bags, Kentucky fried chicken boxes and two plastic bags stuffed with broken bottles and cans.

Beachcombing the following morning, my bare toes narrowly missed a jagged, free-form broken glass sculpture soaring skyward in the grass. I watched flies fighting over ketchup-bedecked paper plates, counted two empty lighter fluid cans, five paper cups, fifteen beer and soda cans, eleven styrofoam cups and more jagged glass in one dune cache fewer than fifty feet away from a half-filled trash can.

Where, in the early morning, the sand had been swept into graceful black and gold designs by the tide, I happened on torn sneakers, a stack of corn husks and a pink leather belt.

As I trudged back across the dunes, midsummer beach-combing over, butterflies danced over the black-eyed Susans around whose stalks Monopoly money was caught.

I suppose when autumn comes, strong waves will sweep Katama clean again, and wind will blow away the striped and mottled cups and spattered plates and sticky plastic bags. And then, perhaps, it will be pleasant to dig my toes into the sand again and look for driftwood planks and follow bird tracks and gather purple beach plums. For I would not want the litter to drive me from this Island that I love.

Hiram Haydn
Talks
About
Editing

I am always struck by the number of authors and editors who are here—William Styron, John Hersey, Lillian Hellman, John Updike, Thornton Wilder, to name a few. Ordinarily, it is as summer visitors that they come, but every now and then one arrives early in the spring, or stays on into the fall, or occasionally through the winter to write in solitude. Hiram Haydn the editor, novelist and critic, is among them.

In 1945, the Haydns first came to Edgartown, and have summered on the Vineyard ever since. Lately, they have stayed at Fishhook, a pre-Civil War dwelling filled with books and willowware, set in a clearing in the Indian Hill woods and rented from fellow writer, Henry Beetle Hough.

A sloping meadow with evergreens constitutes the Haydns'

front yard. Fresh breezes ruffle the field, chickadees chirp and cardinals whistle.

No other distractions exist. The Indian Hill woods are deep and among the loveliest on the Island. On sunny days, the tree boughs meeting above the road paint dancing shadows on the macadam. Then the macadam ends. A dirt lane winds down a hill and Fishhook comes in view.

Most mornings Mr. Haydn can be found seated on a picnic bench on the porch, facing the shingles and working at an old table. He writes with a soft lead pencil on banana-colored paper. When the day's work is done, it is tucked away in the refrigerator—the safest place, he maintains, for a manuscript to be in the event of fire.

Many regard Hiram Haydn as the dean of American editors. Had it not been for his talented eye for recognizing potential, the reading public might never have known—or at least have had a far longer wait before knowing—Reynolds Price, Paule Marshall, William Goldman, Mario Puzo and William Styron. And had it not been for a conspiracy, he might never have been an editor at all, according to the story he told recently while relaxing on the book-strewn porch.

For thirteen years, Mr Haydn recounted, he had been dutifully and satisfiedly teaching at Hawkins Country Day School in Cleveland, Ohio. He had earned a master's degree at Western Reserve. He was doing a little extra night-school teaching and writing. (At the age of eight, he finished his first book—a history of the future—of which he still cherishes six pages.) Then one day a friend urged him to get a doctorate at Columbia University. The idea was appealing, but seemed impossible. Columbia was far away and expensive. But his friend also urged him to apply for a particular fellowship. Hiram Haydn did, and won it.

For his doctoral thesis, he wrote on the philosophers and

thinkers of the late Renaissance whose ideas ran counter to the rationalism and humanism characteristic of that era. (That thesis, in 1950, became a book.)

Because he knew he could only afford to stay at Columbia as long as his fellowship lasted, he worked for two months from 8:00 in the morning until 10:00 at night to complete the thesis.

"I ruined my teeth eating coffee candies for energy," he recollected, "and I lost thirty-five pounds. When I appeared before the board of examiners to defend my work, I looked like an elongated Gandhi. The thesis was enormously long. When you have two months to write a book, you can't cut and be precise. There were a great many young men among the examiners and they wanted to impress the oldsters so they'd ask about things like Footnote 22, and I was in despair. I'd run the race and here I was, but I was afraid I'd be flunked out at the last minute. Then that marvelous man, John Herman Randall, who wrote *The Making of the Modern Mind* and was among the examiners, was called on to make a comment. 'I have said nothing,' he said, 'because I choose to disassociate myself from the frivolity of this examination. This young man has written a book. How many times do we have a dissertation that is a book? This young man is tired. I suggest that we ask him to leave the room so we can confer the degree of Doctor of Philosophy upon him.' They only kept me waiting thirty seconds."

It was not until five years later that Mr. Haydn learned that there had never been any genuine fellowship to send him to Columbia—that the award had been conjured up by his friends, and the money for it provided by Frances P. Bolton, a well-to-do Ohio state representative.

"They cooked it all up to get me moving. Even the headmaster at Hawkins was in on it! He refused to let me go back to Hawkins. At the time, I was in an absolute fury. I knew I'd done a good job. I couldn't understand it. But he realized, too, that it was better for me to move on, so I went to the University of North Carolina to teach English in the Women's College.

After two years there, Mr. Haydn was asked to be executive secretary of the United Chapters of Phi Beta Kappa, and its magazine's editor. Ever since then, he has been an editor—at Crown, Bobbs-Merrill, Random House, Atheneum (of which he was a founder) and Harcourt, Brace and World. Today that firm is Harcourt Brace Jovanovich, with whom he has his own list published under his own colophon—a scorpion with an H in the middle.

Hiram Haydn is also the author of five published novels, and always longs to be writing more fiction. Satisfying as editing is, he finds writing more so. In his last two summers on the Island, he has finished two novels. At this point, however, he began to talk of a few of the recollections to be a part of his memoirs.

He remembered how, when he first worked at Random House, he shared an office with William Faulkner.

"He was a compact little gray-haired man. He sat at a table near me and every time he finished handwriting a page, he'd get up and go over to another table and type it. This went on that first day until noon, and I didn't dare do anything for fear of disturbing him. He was writing *The Town* then. I wouldn't have dreamed of even using the phone. After all, William Faulkner was writing a novel in that room! Finally, I wrote a letter of resignation from Random House in my head. I didn't see what else to do.

"Then, all of a sudden, Faulkner looked up. 'Mr. Haydn,' he said, 'I don't reckon you're hardly doing nothing at all. Use the telephone. See people. You have your work to do and I don't mind.' And from then on, everything was all right. Every morning at 11:30 or 12, he'd turn around and we'd talk. He was really a very charming man. Like Adlai Stevenson, he was a very tiny man, though, and I remember once when he was called on to make a speech, and, to be helpful, someone moved the microphone down to his level. He shot it right up. That was the Confederate general in him. It didn't matter that only the people in the front row could hear him."

Mr. Haydn chuckled, and his brown eyes lit up. Faulkner reminded him of his own novel-writing, and he noted that a writer needs "a certain amount of time to live with a novel. When it's thin, it's because you haven't lived with it enough. I spent eleven years on one book. But there was another one—*Report from the Red Windmill*—that took me only two months.

"As far as reading goes, as an editor, I read a submission very fast. I try to make it as natural an experience as possible—just like reading a book—and I don't want to be either editorial or critical. The question in my mind then is, how much do I want to turn the next page. That's one of my criteria. Then, whenever possible, I take two weeks before I make any definite decision on a submission. I want to see how much of the book is still with me at the end of two weeks, and it's astounding how much, two weeks later, you'll forget."

Mr. Haydn remembers that one of his first "discoveries" as an editor was a young Central American who was working on a farm, but writing, too. "I was so impressed with his talent as a writer—even though his English was awful, he really had something—that I worked with him for two years. Then he sort of disappeared. Several years later, I was at a publication party and a young man came up to me and said, 'Don't you remember me, Maestro?' and it was that same young man. By then, everyone knew him as the director, José Quintero."

Another discovery was Mario Puzo, author of *The God-father,* and a student of Mr. Haydn's at the New School for Social Research.

"I published his *Fortunate Pilgrim.* Then he offered an outline of *The Godfather,* but the company I was with at the time said 'No one wants a novel about the Mafia.' I held out for it for a long time, but I finally had to give in. Afterwards, I couldn't help thinking what a blank-blank I was not to have held out longer.

"Another book I let slip through my fingers and shouldn't have was Mac Hymen's *No Time for Sergeants.* I was at Bobbs-Merrill then. I got a manuscript from a former student and I laughed and I laughed at it, but I took it to one of the other editors to see what he thought. He said, 'You're not usually uncertain. Turn it down.' And that was that."

Mr. Haydn describes himself as a "very editorial editor, not a businessman." Now that publishing companies are being bought by conglomerates whose concern is financial status, he wonders what the future holds for writers.

"I look ahead ten or fifteen years and I wonder if any first novelist will be printed at all. How do you get Faulkners and Nabokovs and Isak Dinesens? They were all young writers once. Their talent was recognized and worked with, but all the big concerns that are buying out publishers today want is money and prestige."

The sun was sinking. Mr. Haydn watched it thoughtfully and tried to remember in how many different Vineyard houses he had vacationed and written and watched the sun set. "I like it best where the deer come up to watch me work," he said.

Autumn
Days

These are golden and russet first fall days. A southwest wind is ruffling the blond and red field grass. Butter-and-eggs, that fragile bell-like weed that, somehow, seems misplaced in fall because of its fragility, is spread across the meadows with the white bouquets of everlasting. Goldenrod glows.

Toadstools of all sizes and shapes are breaking the earth in the woods in their miniature earthquake way. I have always thought of the way that a toadstool ruptures the earth as being a miniature earthquake. There is one under a chestnut in our West Tisbury yard that is ten inches in diameter—a creamy top, edged in rich, velvety brown. It is most regal and serene now in appearance. But what a terrible heaving of earth and leaves there must have been when it thundered its way from underground! And how the ants must have scurried!

Indian pipes are everywhere now, too, in wooded places, their stems wax-white and flamingo-pink. I have noticed now that I have been watching, rather to my surprise, that along with the golds and the rusts of these days there is actually considerable pink, like the Indian pipe, at the end of summer. There are pink shades in grass. There is pink-purple clover. Tiny field asters are all sorts of pink and lavender shades. There are still occasional wild roses blossoming deep pink. Beach plums speckle the dunes with their pink-purple.

In a week or two, I suppose these will all be gone. These languid post-summer days will have turned to fresh, frosty ones where there is no veil of haze over morning skies and no need for foghorns—when the sky will be a bright blue with huge white clouds scudding in dry northeast weather.

There will be crisp grass and crisp leaves underfoot, and the crimsons of poison ivy and sumac that are just starting now to add dash to the roadsides will be everywhere. The wasps are coming indoors to herald this change in the seasons, lying groggily by the stove and in the sun on the windowsills.

The Canada geese, for a month or more, have been suggesting that cold days are coming—flying in great swathes from West Tisbury fields where the grain is ripe to ponds for overnight replenishing of their strength.

And today, from the old Tashmoo pumping station grounds where I had gone to see how many ducks there might be, I saw Craig Kingsbury's wild turkeys strutting in the distance. Thanksgiving, I realized, and it gave me pause, is not that far away.

But the summer has so barely ended, it seems unfair! Not all wicker porch rockers are yet indoors. It is still too early to turn off water in summer cottages, though shutters along East and West Chop and in the Camp Ground, one by one, are beginning to be closed. Boats are being tugged up on ways. What events will have occurred, I wonder, before the boats are caulked and launched for a new summer.

For the young, the end of a summer, although it brings the claustrophobia and rigidity of classrooms, is temporary. When the bicycle is put away and the sand shaken from swimsuits, it is with full expectation that summer will come again soon, even if, before it does, there is winter.

The moment may be miserable, but the future is filled with events.

But for those who are older, listening to the rustle of a favorite oak, putting the mothballs and mouse seed on paper plates, and stripping the beds down to their striped ticking, is a distinctly melancholy time. What shadows will have fallen before the shutters are unshuttered again?

For them, I think, sun and warmth at this time of year is especially soothing (and it has been extraordinarily warm these last few days). One is inclined to be mesmerized into forgetting that winter is not far away.

Although the green horse chestnut cases are falling on Edgartown streets, and store windows, one by one, are being emptied of canvas shoes and gay plaid jackets, it is not yet too cold to go swimming, or picnicking, or bicycling on roads where one no longer need fear the cars.

The fragrances in the early fall air are spicier than in midsummer, but they are still seductive.

The shadows are longer; the sunset sky blazes earlier. Darkness swoops in before 7 P.M. But the crickets still abound and songbirds still sing merrily.

Although winter lies ahead, perhaps it will not be gloomy, after all, and June daisies will be gracing grassy fields before one knows it.

The
Ice Cream
Cow

Down the road about two miles in North Tisbury is the Red Cat Bookstore, just across the way from Argie Humphrey's Bakeshop, where they are advertising for beach plums this week at $25 a bushel. Between the two of them, bakeshop and bookstore, they make that North Tisbury corner a most tempting place to stop—always an abundance of books to browse in, while, from across the way, waft those sweet fragrances of bread-baking and jelly-simmering.

The bookstore is in a rambling sort of house, with an empty field with a giant gnarled oak beside it. When I was a child, a summer visitor to the Vineyard, there was always a brown and white cow chewing grass under the tree, and a thin old man and a roundish old woman made and sold ice cream in the house. But my father always insisted that the cow not only chewed grass like ordinary cows, but lapped cocoa when she was thirsty, and munched peaches and strawberries, and coffee and vanilla beans to flavor her ice cream. He always said that it was he who had discovered her and given her to the old man and old woman. Needless to say, this tale made stopping for ice cream, and patting the cow, every bit as tempting as stopping at the bookstore is nowadays.

My father said he had first met the cow when he was swimming at Lambert's Cove one day.

There he was in the water, he said, splashing and kicking, when all of a sudden he saw a great big brown and white head and two big brown eyes pop up in the water beside him. Of course, he was frightened and shouted "Help," sure that there was a sea serpent beside him ready to gobble him up. But instead of roaring the way a sea serpent would have, the great furry creature said "Moo," and smiled. Then she swam to the shore and walked out of the water, shaking herself all over the way a shaggy dog does.

My father swam after her, of course, because he was curious. By this time, she had walked up to the beach grass and was chewing some. My father said he decided, looking at her, that she must be a sea cow (he didn't know exactly what they looked like but he'd heard about them), and he had, after all, met her in the water. He said there was a little seaweed on her back, which he took off, and he patted her nose and she looked pleased.

He said he talked to the cow for a while and asked her if she would like to play Blind Man's Buff in the water (which was my father's favorite water game). She seemed to agree that that would be fun, even though it is hard for only two to play, and they did play for a while. Then it got to be time to go home, my father said, and he didn't know what to do with the cow. It was much too long a run for her to follow his bicycle to East Chop, it was getting late and cold, and the cow was shivering and she didn't seem to want to go back into the water.

Then, my father said, he remembered the oak tree in North Tisbury, which was the sort of tree that looked as if a cow belonged under it. He asked the cow if she would like an oak tree to graze beneath, and the cow mooed; he guessed that that meant yes, so he told her he would ride slowly and she was to follow his bicycle.

She ambled along very nicely after the bicycle, he said, and when they got to the yellow house where the old man and the old woman lived, she waited quietly outside the door and didn't try to get in or climb over the fence to sit under the oak tree. She flicked her tail once or twice when a fly came by, but she was very patient.

My father said he knocked on the door and the old woman answered.

He said he asked her if she'd like a pretty brown and white cow that wanted an oak tree to sit under.

The old woman said, "Cow?"

And the old man said, "Cow?"

And the old woman said they didn't have any use for a cow.

That was when my father told them that his cow wasn't an ordinary cow.

He said he started to tell them how she had come out of the water with seaweed on her back, but then he thought better of that.

He said he was scratching his head and trying to think of something special the cow did—like playing Blind Man's Buff, except that that probably wouldn't appeal to old people—

when he noticed that the old man was eating a dish of ice cream.

"This is an ice cream cow," my father said.

"An ice cream cow?" the man said.

"An extraordinary ice cream cow," my father said.

"She makes chocolate ice cream and vanilla ice cream and probably strawberry and peach ice cream, too. It depends on what you feed her," my father said he continued. "For example," he said, "I like vanilla ice cream on Mondays, so I feed her vanilla beans every Monday morning and by suppertime I have vanilla ice cream. And on Tuesdays I feed her coffee beans for breakfast because I like coffee ice cream on Tuesdays.

"Of course, she eats hay and grass in between times," my father said. He said when he told me the story that, of course, he didn't really think the cow was an ice cream cow, but he thought maybe the old man and the old woman would take her if they thought she was an ice cream cow, and then, after a while, even if she didn't give ice cream but only milk, they would have grown fond of her and would keep her.

Sure enough, he said, they decided to keep her.

The old man came out of the house and walked around her and looked at her.

The cow sat very still, smiled and didn't even say "Moo."

The old man said, "She doesn't look like an ice cream cow."

But my father said, "Did you ever see any other cow who smiled like that?"

The old man admitted he never had.

The old woman agreed she never had.

My father said he would have asked the cow to give ice cream for them except that it was late in the day and she was tired.

The old man said, all right, he guessed she could stay. If she didn't give ice cream she certainly ought to give milk and he could sell her.

My father said he thanked them very much, and said he was sure the cow would enjoy living with them, particularly since she liked oak trees so much. He said he would come and visit her now and then. He patted the cow on the nose, he said, and got on his bicycle and rode back down to East Chop.

Of course, he said, it was a long time before he had the courage to go back to see the cow after the story he'd told about her that he knew wasn't true.

But one day, he said, he was riding his bicycle on the road in North Tisbury and went past the yellow house, and there was a crowd of people outside, all eating ice cream in paper cups with wooden spoons.

He said some of them were eating vanilla ice cream and some of them were eating chocolate ice cream and some of them were eating strawberry ice cream and some of them were eating peach ice cream. He said he looked over the fence and there sat his cow, as pretty as you please, with a pink bow around her neck and three pails in front of her. One pail said coffee beans, one pail said cocoa and one pail said vanilla beans, he said.

The cow saw him, he said, and came right over. He guessed she was chewing coffee beans at the time because she smelled like a percolator.

She smiled at him and mooed, and put one hoof out for him to shake the way a dog does, and all the people eating ice cream stopped eating ice cream and watched and were very impressed.

And the old man and the old woman inside the yellow house saw that all the people outside had stopped eating ice cream and came out to see what was the matter. And when they saw that it was the boy who had given them the cow, my father said, they came running up and clapped him on the back and thanked him for bringing them such a wonderful cow.

And the old man went into the house and came out with a silver dish piled high with ice cream, and asked my father if he had any idea where they could find another ice cream cow.

My father was a little frightened, he said. It was all so strange, the way the cow had really turned into an ice cream cow. But he said the ice cream was delicious, and the cow was very happy under the oak tree, and certainly well fed. And the old man and the old woman said he could have free ice cream anytime he wanted it—any flavor. So he said he used to go back to see the cow and have ice cream at least once a week after that.

Shutting Down

In autumn on the Vineyard, I am noticing, people leave and animals return.

It was June when I last saw a deer, but now that October is here and Labor Day is past, they are browsing again in the scrub oak and bounding—white tails in the air—across up-Island roads. Ten quail were noticed marching across a Chilmark lawn the other day. Rabbits are abroad again. Emmett Carroll's guinea hens, emboldened by the absence of traffic, seem to be having a most pleasant time seeking out fat bugs to eat on the Middle Road.

The honking of Canada geese quitting ponds after a restful night's bobbing awakens me each morning at 6:00 o'clock.

But otherwise, it is almost soundless in mid-Island now—a

welcome respite after the wheezing of tourist buses and the summer-long roar of speeding cars.

In town, admittedly, there is a certain ghostly quality now that the visitors have left. Most shop windows are empty, with soap swirls on the glass to deflect the glances of the over-curious. There are no longer posted menus outside restaurant doors tantalizing with suggestions of broiled native swordfish and quahaug chowder. If you peer hopefully through the windows of the Edgartown Dairy Queen, there are only empty ice cream cup cartons and, looking abandoned, those fat shiny machines that, in midsummer, so endlessly spouted frozen custard in glistening peaks.

In Oak Bluffs, there are no hot popcorn smells on Circuit Avenue. Most of the curio shops, offering seahorse-shaped combs, writhing paper snakes on sticks, feather headdresses and seashell ashtrays, are closed.

Around East Chop, the shuttered windows are like so many great green eyes—and porch chairs are all standing on their heads with their bottoms exposed.

The rafts for boat mooring have been pulled up along Lake Anthony. Only a handful of masts now sprout from Edgartown harbor waters and yacht club precincts echo as you walk through them.

At Menemsha, Rasmus Klimm has taken in his smiling sea serpents and gone back to the Cape for the winter. The art galleries and the antique shops are emptied of their wares; only Beetlebung remains open, fragrant with cucumber soaps and bayberry candles. And the lobster tanks are still bubbling at the fish markets.

In the way of fragrance in the fall, there are pungent wild grapes and beach plums. There are bayberry, sweet fern, the sweetness of fallen apples and the clean smell of zinnias and marigolds.

Blue jays are back in full force now, along with the quail and the deer, and there are no summer people competing with their outspoken scolding.

Pleased as I am with most aspects of fall, the abundance of insect life now is not all appealing. I have been reading Jean Henri Fabre, but it does no good. Only the crickets that pop into the house whenever a door is opened these days are not distasteful, though their sudden movements have been known to make me jump. But I have no use for the sinister black spiders, buzzing horseflies and omnipresent fruit flies that nestle in corners or hover in the kitchen. I was sent a *Life of the Spider* by a friend not long ago, for he was eager to have me appreciate all aspects of nature, but the hairy arachnid whose picture (supposedly invitingly) decorates the cover is so lifelike that I keep the book in a wrapper at all times.

On the whole, though, the country fall is captivating. There is a loneliness to it at a summer resort, certainly, and that melancholy, thought-provoking aura of the end of life. But yesterday I walked the Gay Head beach and the air was crisp and cool; the beach so clean of any but natural debris—dogfish flung up in a high tide, orange-red starfish—that I felt as if the beach were all my beach again, a feeling I have not had since June.

A few days earlier, the white, smooth sand of Lambert's Cove belonged to me in late afternoon, with a gold-streaked sky overhead and jade-green water stretching toward Naushon.

In fall, the Vineyard is entirely mine, somehow—mine and the animals'. And so, in summertime I do not covet hilltop homes of seasonal visitors. Shop windows look derelict now. Shuttered houses are mournful. But they can be overlooked when one knows soon one will have an Island all one's own.

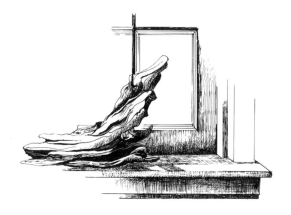

Vance Packard
Speaking

The other day I went to Chappaquiddick to see the Vance Packards. I took the ferry about mid-morning when the sun was glistening on Edgartown harbor. Four busy mallards were swimming near the town wharf and hoping for a handout, but since school has begun, there are no youthful fishermen on the dock with sandwiches to share. So there were impatient squawks as the birds paddled about, sizing up each newcomer to the waterfront with an eye particularly on his pockets and the quantity of bread they might hold.

At this time of year, there are only a handful of families on Chappaquiddick, and Jerry Grant who runs the ferry, or John Willoughby who assists him, is likely to ask who you are off to see on the little island of juniper and scrub oak and sassafras—not to pry, but to make sure the trip is not made in vain, for they always know who has crossed over that day.

I was assured as I boarded the two-car ferry (which on my trip was carless) that the Packards were in.

They were to meet me at the ferry landing, but I had a while to wait, so I walked up the road past Adrian Lamb's gracious waterfront house, just closed for the season, and onto his beach. We have met once or twice and are well enough acquainted so that he will stop on Main Street to talk of the sea gulls he has befriended and worries about when he returns to Connecticut for the winter. One, in particular, he says, always waits and watches when he goes fishing, expectant that when his catch is cleaned, something tasty will be left on a beach spile.

There were black-backed gulls aplenty bobbing near the shore, but they continued to bob, oblivious of my beach stroll.

I returned to the road and walked on as far as Caleb's Pond pausing to pick a few rose hips in their furry leaves, before I turned back toward the ferry and found Mr. Packard.

We drove down the main road again and then turned off onto a dirt one. At its end, the Packards' Victorian house sprawled. Whale's vertebra decorated the yard—only a suggestion, it turned out, of the eclectic furnishings that were to be found inside—a stylish bookcase fashioned from an old ice chest; a coffee table that was once a hatch cover; and a dining room table that cost $5 at a Chilmark fire sale.

A treadle sewing machine had been transformed into a dressing table. Room dividers were fish nets. Bleached driftwood decorated lintels and, on the stair dividers, the lady of the house had painted all the important events in their family history—births, marriages and graduations—in gay colors.

Among those notable events was the arrival three decades ago of the Vance Packards on the Vineyard.

In those days, Vance Packard was not a social critic. He was not the best-selling writer of *The Status Seekers, The Hidden Persuaders, The Pyramid Climbers,* and *The Sexual Wilderness.* He was a young journalist who came to the Vineyard to teach his wife to bicycle, and who quickly decided that the Island was to be, forever, a special place for him.

While we were talking, we sat on their sunny porch watching the autumn wind shift shadows in the bending beach grass, and both the Packards reminisced about the Vineyard they had known, about boating and bluefishing and beachcombing, and the conduciveness of the Island to writing best-selling works.

In keeping with the setting, the Packards looked ruddy and healthy and happy, both in bulky white sweaters; he in a nautical cap and she in a yellow babushka. Mr. Packard has light blue eyes that go with a hazy Island sky. Mrs. Packard's eyes complement the sea in green moods.

"Our first summer on the Vineyard was our best summer," Mrs. Packard recalled nostalgically. "I remember we'd go down to the beach and stay all day and do our washing on a scrubbing board, and then we'd come home when we felt like it, and it was perfectly marvelous."

"I think what she means," suggested Mr. Packard, "is that we weren't caught up in the cocktail circuit yet. Nowadays, there's always that problem. The best time to go bluefishing is in the twilight, and that's the cocktail hour, too, so you have to make a choice."

"And in the old days, we used to do more sailing," Mrs. Packard continued, caught up in her reverie. "Remember, Vance, the day that our TEK dinghy came was the same day the telegram arrived from *American* magazine saying that it was closing and you were out of a job?"

"So I switched over to *Collier's,* and in three months that was over, too, just a few days before Christmas in 1956. That was quite a time in our lives. We were trying to hold onto our house in Darien, but after all, I was out of work and we didn't see how we could. We were turning off lights all the time and blocking off rooms to save electricity and fuel and we were trying to keep the children from knowing, and then, one night, one of them came to us and offered fifty-seven cents to help out. I guess we hadn't done a very good job of keeping things to ourselves.

"But all the same, I kept on dreaming," Mr. Packard said. "I'd been doing research on *The Hidden Persuaders* when I was on the *American,* and I'd submitted the manuscript to a publisher, so I could daydream and figure out how much it would bring us if I sold, say, 12,000 copies. I couldn't imagine a book's selling more than 12,000 copies."

Mrs. Packard smiled. "But it did," she recollected. "It sold 150,000 in hardcover alone. The sleeper of 1957, they called it."

And since then, Vance Packard has been free-lancing. When it is on the Vineyard rather than in Connecticut that he is working, he gets up at 7:30, takes a quick swim at the beach below his house, eats a breakfast of English muffins and cheese, and retires to his office with a thermos of coffee and the intention, at least, of working until 1:30—unless the temptations of watching wild turkeys and deer in the field under his office window prove too great. The Packards always come to the Vineyard with cartons of notes that need culling and they all remain in their cartons encircling the study while they are being worked upon.

"That's why we always have to make two trips from New

Canaan," Mrs. Packard sighed. "He keeps telling me about neighbors who come here with two suitcases for the summer and asking why I can't pack like that. But he always has to travel with everything. When he was writing *The Status Seekers,* even though we went to Europe and visited eleven countries, Vance never saw anything until night, he kept so busy."

"But I saw the outside of every museum in Europe."

"That was the time," Mrs. Packard remembered, "when we started out with eleven pieces of luggage and three children. We came back with the same three children, but with twenty-five pieces of luggage! The awfullest assorted pieces of luggage you ever saw in your life! String bags and everything. We kept them tied on top of the Peugeot when we were traveling. There was no room for them anyplace else, so whenever we stopped at a restaurant we had to sit near the window so we could keep our eyes on them, and at night that awful assortment had to be carried into every hotel."

Where he writes is of relatively little importance to Vance Packard, he explained, but where he organizes the material he will use is of utmost importance. He finds the Vineyard one of the most favorable places for that.

"How do I organize? Well, I have a box and all new material that comes in goes into the box, and I keep adding and adding and adding to it. It's awfully difficult, you know, to end research. You can say to yourself, 'Stop, I have enough now,' and start organizing, but all the time you keep on seeing new things, so you have to keep adding. Most books take me two to two and a half years to do. Probably two-thirds of the time is spent organizing."

Ever since he began writing exposés of American problems, his mailbox, as well as his head, has been full of ideas.

"There always seem to be plenty of people with plenty of ideas for me."

As for those that he has himself, "On the last go-round I had about six possibilities in mind. I tried them all out on members of the family and close friends. Then I decided, no matter what I chose, I was going to offend somebody. So—in the quiet of my study, as Mr. Nixon does, you know, I made the decision myself. It was based on what I thought I would most enjoy researching for the next two or three years."

Just then a bird fluttered in the grass outside. Mr. Packard jumped up to watch it, to look out at the distant Katama sands and recall the days in World War II when he and his wife had just bought the house and their beach was littered with abandoned Navy material.

"Why, there were years when we operated a lumberyard here," Mr. Packard said. "All the lumber from the whole damn ocean and the Navy and everything would come right up on our beach and the boys and I would go down to collect it.

"Now just look at the way that bluff is starting to turn red," Mr. Packard said pensively, watching the land between the house and the sea. "You get such beautiful oranges and reds here. And look at the wind in the grass."

All social commentary was forgotten as the scene before him was contemplated, and the topic turned to neighbors and life on the Island, and the wind songs one could make with Aeolian harps. Mrs. Packard went in search of one, and then in search of a window that would afford the right breeze for the strings of the strange instrument.

"There," he said satisfiedly, when the right spot had been found. "Now isn't that lovely?"

Hunting
Season

It is deer season, and wherever one goes on the roads this week there are cars full of crimson-costumed hunters. They come in four-wheel-drive cars and sleek black sedans. The estimate is that 150 of them are here from off-Island, appetites whetted for the kill. This morning, as I drove to Edgartown, they were clustered by the airport underbrush and below the Matthiessen farm. They were readying their shotguns, loading them and closing them with ominous snapping sounds that echoed and re-echoed in the still woods.

I have seen several deer this fall, and the killers' presence in such numbers suggests, of course, that they have been told to expect good hunting.

I saw one deer in our field at just about sunrise one

morning—a slender doe munching on a pine. At Dugans' at Indian Hill, they have nipped at the evergreens with such precision that three trees in the front yard look as if they had been perfectly pruned for a topiary. The others that I have seen have been bedazzled by car lights on the road at night; one, nestled in a bed of leaves by the roadside, in a most fetching way. Another took me quite by surprise on a walk up Peaked Hill toward dusk one afternoon. At 298 feet, this is the Island's second highest site. From it, one can look off through green-gold pines and deep green spruces to Vineyard Sound and the Atlantic.

There are almost no sounds there in fall but the wind rustling dry trees and tall blond grass and purple sumac, and the waves of the Atlantic rolling in the distance. Occasionally, a deer mouse, long ears quivering, scampers among fallen scrub oak tree leaves, or a crow caws, or a squirrel, unnerved by a passerby, plummets without meaning to from a squirrel-gray branch to the unprotective ground. But otherwise it is still.

I walked up the hill on an afternoon when sunset puffs of gold were here and there among scudding, darkening clouds. The water was gray-green, the air soft for a fall afternoon, and I looked out toward the sea and Sound. When I turned back toward the road, standing beside it was a six-point buck, regal, imposing, white-tailed, white-chested and surely stuffed. I smiled and wondered what whimsical Vineyarder had put it in such a perfect Museum of Natural History setting—on a hilltop with water in the distance, wheat-like grass and ruby-red rose hips, and squirrels and mice as background fauna. I began to walk nearer to look more closely when suddenly there was a shiver of the tawny hide, and I realized that only four feet away a live buck was standing. We stood a while, face to face—his black nose quivering, his crown of horns silhouetted against the deepening sky. There was neither fright nor ferocity in the dark brown eyes, and, finding neither, I walked past. I turned around once afterward and he was still watching—alert, unafraid on the hilltop, looking out as I had toward the Sound, over the brush, through the evergreens.

On my way down the hill, trailing my scarf in a thicket, something wet touched my hand and when, startled, I looked to see what it had been, I found it was another deer inquisitively examining my palm and licking salt spray gently, methodically, from my fingers.

And so I think that I have ample reason to be shuddering today as I have heard the guns go off.

Mussels
Mariniere
with
Joel Grey

"Hi," Joel Grey said. "Do you mind if I keep on working? I've got some mussels here I'm going to throw in with some garlic and white wine and a little oil in the bottom of a pan. I came up with shredded hands getting them, but it was worth it."

The diminutive Broadway star (he is five feet, five inches tall), acclaimed as the master of ceremonies in the musical *Cabaret* and as George M. Cohan in *George M.,* emerged with a grin from behind the kitchen counter where he had been making preparations for lunch.

He might well have been making a stage entrance as he advanced into the dining room of costume designer Patricia Zipprodt's West Tisbury house, and perched on a milk stool in front of the fireplace. When Joel Grey moves, he dances. His springy, curly hair bounces, and he cocks his head a little to one side.

"I don't hunt, but I mussel," he continued, once ensconced by the fire. "I can regain my patience in just a few days on the Vineyard, and in New York, my patience is always tested and strung out. I love the city. It's one of my favorite places in the whole world, but so many of our human rights are lost there every year. Here, it's so different. This is such a subtle place. There's such a sense of quiet expectation about everyone who comes. It's such an unselfconscious place. A lot of summer communities get a case of the cutes, and this hasn't. Even the old houses aren't spruced up the way a lot of homes of their age and beauty elsewhere would be.

"We're all city kids," Mr. Grey continued, swinging around on the milking stool, "my wife and our children and me. We're all children when it comes to the country. A grouse, field mice, a pheasant, a deer—they're all like terrific events. I walk outside here and I see a thousand beautiful sights. Everywhere you look there's a beautiful photograph by Eliot Porter—or should I say, since he's such a devoted Vineyarder, Alfred Eisenstaedt?"

He grinned again, and popped up from his place by the fire for a quick look at his mussels.

It was early on a Saturday afternoon. Mr. Grey was minding the house while his wife took ten-year-old Jennifer and six-year-old Jimmy horseback riding.

"The kids just absolutely love it here. God, they're learning a lot."

Mr. Grey returned to the milking stool, stroked his pink-sweat-shirted chest and remarked that his first acquaintance with the Vineyard began one day when he thought the

Vineyard was Nantucket, where a red Rover was supposed to be waiting for him at the airport. His plane landed. There was a red Rover waiting and he drove off in it—only to discover he was in the wrong red Rover—on the wrong island. Although, that time, he ended up by going on to Nantucket, his brief glimpse of the Vineyard convinced him that he wanted a longer stay. "And so we've been here every month since August. We came in September, for Columbus Day, and we were here for Thanksgiving. I expect we'll keep on coming, at least some weekends, until February."

Mr. Grey rose again to check the lunch. When he is not dancing across a floor, he is swaggering across one—but making every move graceful, and making sure that it counts.

When he returned, we began to talk theater.

"How did I get started in it? It was when I was ten," he said. "I was one of those kids who always got to school late because I was up late acting the night before. I used to perform with my father, Mickey Katz, the Yiddish comedian. Mind you, I didn't have the sort of stage parents who *made* me perform. I wanted to. But it all ended up by making for a very special kind of childhood that was hard and that I don't look back on with any reverence."

He poked at the fire, and this time squatted tailor-fashion before it to talk of *Cabaret,* the award-winning musical of pre-World War II Berlin decadence that, a few years ago, brought him virtually overnight fame.

"I was in it for a year," he said. "If an actor is in a part any longer than that I don't believe he can grow—at least, I can't. After that, you're just finding energy, not creative spontaneity to contribute to a part, and I feel you have to find some new challenge. Once you stop growing in a role, of course, you're just a piece of mechanics. Sometimes directors are aware of this and, when a play has a long run, they reshape things to give the actors a chance to be spontaneous again. That's why it's always very refreshing in a long-run play when a new person comes in. Then you have a new approach to react to. Too often, though," Mr. Grey said, and his enormous brown eyes looked mournful, "a director makes a new actor do an imitation of the one before.

"I've directed *Cabaret* on tour," Mr. Grey continued, "and I loved working with the actors. If you're a thinking actor, you think somewhat in directional terms, anyway, unless you're just a puppet. But an important part of acting, too, of course, is to know when to let yourself be a puppet. You must both explore the part that you're working on and, at the same time, be totally malleable. You must have a good enough relationship with your director to be able to say, 'Listen, that's no good for me.' And when he says, 'Do it, or else,' that's when plays fail."

Mr. Grey added wood to the fire and solemnly evaluated his art.

"I find acting very hard," he said. "It's almost never that joyful experience that's depicted in Warner Brothers movies. It's very hard, demanding work and it takes a kind of concentration that colors the rest of your life and your day and what your family gets of you. All of your energies, no matter how you try to control them, are directed toward your work. Your family gets only a very small part of you. That's why I made a choice not to work this fall. We all needed to see what life would be like together."

Mr. Grey turned once more to the subject of acting.

"What sorts of parts do I like to play? I like to do things that have intentions, anyway. I like to start out in a play, at least, believing in it. I'd like to do some Shakespeare. I've been invited to do *Hamlet* and *Richard III* at the Cleveland Playhouse and I'm excited about those. The black characters are always more fun to play than the wholesome ones. They're exhausting, but they're fun."

Having sat still for too long, it was time for some stage business. Mr. Grey swept a brown scarf from the back of a chair and wrapped it around his neck. He talked briefly of Broadway and off-Broadway and musical comedy. Musical comedy, in the old sense, he remarked, is a thing of the past. "*Hair* and *Company* are the fresh, exciting sorts of musicals that lie ahead. But, he added, the things that are exciting and relevant are increasingly going to be done off-Broadway and in regional theater.

"But I ought to tell you about my wife, Jo Wilder. She used to be a very, very good actress, and probably still is, but we got married thirteen years ago and she became a housewife and mother, and I think those are very underrated jobs. Mothering and wifing and homemaking are very meaningful jobs. She works a lot harder than any so-called working lady."

The front door opened and banged shut. The pretty, long-haired Grey daughter ran in.

"Excuse me, Daddy, Mommy would like to know if she should get more garlic before she puts the car away?"

Mr. Grey said he thought that would be a good idea, and his daughter whisked out with the message, to return a few minutes later with her small brother.

"I'm starved. Are we going to have lunch soon?" he inquired. "Oh, you have a little fire. Hello, cute little fire," and he approached it happily.

"Do you want to talk to that fire?" his father asked.

"Of course," was the matter-of-fact reply. "Last night we had a fire, too, and we roasted marshmallows and I won double bingo."

"Want some orange juice?" inquired the father.

"Ummm," Jimmy thought for a while. "We have some swan food," he said unexpectedly. "We stopped to feed the swans on the Mill Pond when we were on our way home."

"Jimmy, what are those knitting needles doing in that vaseful of wheat?" his father inquired, studying the bouquet in the center of the table.

"Hmm? Oh, those. Oh, I was making a nest."

Clearly mystified, Mr. Grey changed the subject and asked his daughter how the riding lesson had been.

"Terrific," was the reply. "And tomorrow, do you know what we're going to do? Tomorrow, we're going to take our horses up in back of the Agricultural Hall to ride them.

"Daddy, I'm hungry. Are we having mussels? Do you want me to set the table? Do we need knives? How about nutcrackers?"

When I left, a lively family afternoon was in full swing at the Greys'.

Snow
Walk

Although I have often spent winters in snow country, in school in New Hampshire and Switzerland and Massachusetts' Connecticut River Valley, I have never ceased to wonder at the magic of snow, whether it is angry and wind-tossed or gentle and soft.

Only once before this winter had I seen the Island in snow—Oak Bluffs' gingerbread houses with frosted peaks; the grass on Chilmark moors amber against the white; Moshup's Trail a taffeta ribbon shimmering silver under a midmorning sun.

One Christmas when I was a child, I visited on the Vineyard and slept in a gabled room. That was the time when I first glimpsed snow on the Island. I remember there was a special excitement to being protectively under a gable watching William Street lengthen and widen beneath my eyes the way everything lengthens and widens in snow.

That, of course, is one of the most magical qualities of a snowfall. Then the world seems to expand. Shadows stretch. There are no roads until a plow passes. Fields, ponds, hills, highways, all converge.

Last night, while the snow was still falling—fine, dry powder sifting down in front of street lights—I went for a walk down Music Street to the Middle Road; down the South Road to Chilmark, where the Tiasquin bubbles. The silence that the snow brings muffles soft sounds, but somehow sharpens the clear ones. Church bells and cowbells and sleigh bells, the barking of dogs, tumbling brooks—all are brought closer by a snowfall. At 9:00 o'clock the Congregational Church clock struck the hour. By then, I was at the Middle Road, but the sound of the clock seemed so near that, at the first toll, I jumped.

I remembered a night in the Austrian Alps when, similarly, I was walking in falling snow. I had been passing the village's church when the bell in its onion dome started to ring. I had stopped short with a start, and a passerby had hailed me and asked me to stop at the inn for a drink.

He was, it turned out, the mayor of the Austrian village, and a German Army veteran of World War II. Late into the snowy night, he talked in English with a Southern drawl of having been a prisoner of war in America, and of the black sergeant who had been his guard. He recalled the summer day years later when, back in his Alpine village, he had looked out the town hall window to see a black man with a jaunty Tyrolean hat bicycling down the street. There was something familiar in the toss of the head. He raised the window and shouted in English to the cyclist, and the man looked up—it was the black sergeant who had been his guard and tutor in English.

That is another of the magical qualities of a snowy night. It is conducive to reminiscences like that. There is something, also, about snow that makes one friendly and expansive.

Last night I smelled sweet wood smoke as I passed one house tucked behind pines whose limbs were weighted with snow blossoms—rather like giant white chrysanthemums they seemed in the dark. The smoke tickled my nostrils. Sounds of life in the yard piqued my curiosity. I stopped to listen and to look, for in the dim light an animal seemed to be pawing. There turned out to be not only a dog—an elderly, waddling one taking a constitutional—but his mistress, as well, shoveling a path. And we stopped and talked for quite some time, though we are more neighbors than genuine acquaintances.

Once, on my walk, an avenue of evergreens frightened me. It was not that they were thickly planted, but I think it was the contrast of their green-blackness against the glistening white that dismayed me. All around, the world was so full of light I wanted everything to be.

I expect I walked two miles or more before I started back. Walks in the snow, like walks along a beach, make one forgetful of time. A snowscape is without the landmarks we are used to seeing. The shapes of houses and barns and sheds are altered. Bends in roads disappear. It is easy to be lost in a snowfall because of the way it transforms familiar shapes.

This morning, I was out again. I was later than the birds—the mass of them that come to feed at our kitchen window, cracking sunflower seeds with hard taps on the wood. But there were still a few late-rising chartreuse-breasted evening grosbeaks, each disguised by a black domino hiding its eyes.

And the crows—like shadows looming—waited on the

branch of an elm tree to have bread scattered for them. Buntings and sparrows darted to and fro. A woodpecker drummed on a dead pine and the chips he dislodged made hollows in the snow.

I had never noticed before how colors, like sounds and shapes, are metamorphosed by the snow. Pink appears in the gray of bark that never seemed pink before. The moss under a ledge is gray-green, where on snowless days it is dusty green. Rocky stream beds glint bronze; thickets are russet. There are nut-browns and sand-browns and tawny camel shades in grass and brush against snow.

After my morning wanderings among the birds and trees, I set off toward Gay Head this afternoon to see how it had fared in the storm. The cliffs were like a marble cake dusted with powdered sugar; the Elizabeth Islands stretched like the paws of a silver fox.

On my way back, I stopped to watch the ducks in Quitsa Pond, scurrying out of the way of miniature ice floes. Elsewhere, smaller ponds were frozen and wind-driven snow had made swirling patterns on them.

Down-Island, cars and people apparently had melted the snowfall sooner than on less traveled up-Island routes, but the magic was not entirely missing. In Edgartown, I chuckled at elegant Water Street homes looking as if they had been made sway-backed by the snow driven against the eaves.

And here and there, I have been stopping to study the animal tracks. I think I saw round rabbit paw prints by the Garden Club, and I wondered if it was a mouse that had left the untidy, uneven marks that trailed off into the woods.

There was a snowfall in New York on Christmas Eve two years ago, and I remember how the city rested under it. Only children and a few churchgoers were out. Even the plows, till early morning, were still. But then, with morning, came the flood of people and the lines of cars. The streets were slate-gray slush by noon, and artificial Christmas trees with stiff green limbs and painted tinsel already were littering the streets. But here, today, the snow is still as pure as it was yesterday. The air is crisp and clear. The wind is fresh. I am enjoying this country living.

An
Account
of
Eeling

I have just been eeling. Sadly, I must admit to failure in every aspect of that endeavor.

I chopped no hole in the ice. I caught no eels. Worse yet, although I cadged four eels from my more successful companion, I could not even peel them.

All I have done is cook and eat them, basic rather than commendatory acts.

It all began because of this week's plummeting temperatures and the ice on virtually every Island pond. Passing Sengekontacket on Tuesday, I saw buckets and baskets and sacks spread on the ice, and men in waders and yellow slickers wielding axes. At lunchtime, talking with an Ocean Heights resident, I learned that her husband went eeling.

When I expressed interest in the operation, she said perhaps I'd like to join him. She told me he would be going out on the ice again in about an hour.

I quickly had to rig myself out in borrowed finery. When I told friends I was off on an eeling expedition in nylons and a miniskirt, they gasped, and one, being a duck hunter, moaned at the cold I would suffer advancing on the ice so skimpily clad. So I called someone about my size and asked her, since she was a doctor's wife and should know all about how to maintain the proper body temperature, what she would advise if I were going eeling.

"Red thermal underwear," she said. (No explanation was ever forthcoming as to why it needed to be red.) "An anorak with a hood, suitable for cold climates, designed for Arctic exploration. Ski socks and double-knit mittens."

That equipment, she concluded, after she had supplied it and examined me from head to toe, poking to see if there were sufficient clothing layers, seemed quite adequate.

And so I ventured forth.

Lewis Hathaway, Jr., who had volunteered to be my guide, kindly took me by the hand as we advanced out onto the ice. But it did little good. There was a splat, and I fell. I rubbed an icy shin. He asked if I were sure I was all right. I assured him I was. When I was on my feet again he suggested that, rather than selecting the slickest, shiniest patches of ice to step on, I look for the little snow blossoms on the surface. They made surer footing, he said.

So we advanced some more.

Across the pond, the men with baskets and burlap bags and boxes were hacking their eel-fishing holes. I started to ask if we would join them. Then I noticed a streak of sloshing water between them and us that gave me pause. That was when I asked how thick the ice was. Mr. Hathaway tapped with his axe once or twice. Then he began chopping an eeling hole, and said he guessed it was three to three and a half inches thick. I nervously compared that with things I knew. I estimated it wasn't even the thickness of a Dagwood sandwich.

I inquired about the depth of the water beneath. Mr. Hathaway peered into the black hole he had just cut, and said it was probably about six feet deep where we were.

"Oh," I said.

Meanwhile, Mr. Hathaway was poking an extra-long garden-rake-like thing that he explained was an eel spear into the hole and was jabbing it into the mud.

"Nothing to this," he said. "You just keep circling and jabbing with your spear. You can even find a hole another fellow thinks is all fished out, but it won't be because you spear on another angle and get the eels he missed."

That was when he caught the first one—one foot long, writhing and yellow-bellied. It whipped in muddy circles on the ice for a while. Mr. Hathaway told me to take a look at its glazed eyes, so I'd get an idea how sleepy it was. Hibernating eels, he explained, frequently develop an unappetizing scum over their eyes in winter, since there is no reason for keen vision then. He added, as I painfully watched the eel's gyrations, that I needn't worry about whether it was suffering or not. It was too dozy to feel very much. And it would freeze so quickly on the ice and in the open air, it wouldn't know what had hit it.

After a while, I asked if I might use his spear.

He was more than agreeable about it. He told me to simply shuffle rhythmically about and jab into the mud as he'd been jabbing.

With the first jab, I thought I was a goner. Spear and I together, I suspected, were about to be sucked into the mud.

For although I heard no gurgling sound below, I felt the endless squish and ooze of mud. The spear went deep and deeper. I danced perilously close to the hole edge to try to pull it out. Mr. Hathaway, who was taking time out for a cigarette, had to give up his smoking and come to the rescue.

He pushed and pulled in the hole a while longer. He explained that rarely is an eel actually speared. More often, it is caught between the tines of the spear-like fork. He caught four eels before he moved on, leaving them in loops and S's on the ice. I was told that when we had fished our fill, we would come back to collect them all.

We eeled in four holes altogether. When luck didn't seem to be with us, we would start off in a brand new direction on the ice. Mr. Hathaway said you should move in the direction in which you find the most eels. He said best eeling spots differ from year to year. He added that, long ago, the Island had many more eels. (An eelgrass disease in 1931 was responsible for the disappearance of some of the eels, as well as all sorts of other fish and many birds, I later learned. Brant, codfish, scallops, crabs—all began to thin out as the eelgrass, killed in some mysterious way, became more and more sparse. The grass was the first link in a food chain for larger fish and animals and was a beloved nesting place for eels. Although there is a good deal more eelgrass now than there was in those dark days, it has never grown back quite so abundantly as before.)

I eeled once more, for a few moments, but it was no use. There was the same glub-glub effect as before, and the spear went deeper and deeper without my feeling the tug of any eel. I did come up, however, with a winsome baby flounder that had to be thrown back quickly before it froze, a sea cucumber split in two by the spear and an ugly, thick-lipped eel pout.

We stayed out about two hours. By that time, for all the beauty of blue sky and blue ice and ducks and geese overhead, I was too blue with cold to be properly appreciative. Mr. Hathaway gathered up the eels he had strewn about and we slipped and slid back toward his house.

He told me, en route, that if I wished to eel again perhaps I would like to put cleats of some kind on the soles of my boots, so I would be steadier on my feet. He said small pieces of chain were affixed by some to boot bottoms for that purpose.

Back on land, he offered me an eel or two if I would like them—provided I thought I could find someone else to do the skinning. He said he always gave his eels away rather than skin them. He explained that they are slick with slime and that this makes them hard to grasp to clean. He said some people nailed their eels to a wall to skin them; others laid them out on a paper, slit their throats and stomachs and peeled back their skins with a bit of burlap bag, or, if the going got rough, with a pair of pliers. He said the most important thing was to get the skin off whole. He began to reminisce about some of the fine eel skinners of his boyhood who could peel an eel in less than three minutes.

"There was one man," he said, "used to grab them in his teeth by their heads, and then he'd yank and yank and as long as you had a tub of salt water handy for the eels and plenty of beer for him, he'd keep at it."

It was growing late. I thanked him for my eeling expedition, inquired if the frozen eels were likely to limber up in the heat of the car as I carried them home (I said I wouldn't want them wriggling in the back seat), and when I was informed that I need not worry, set off.

Back in West Tisbury, I went up to Alley's General Store, for surely, I thought, there would be an eel skinner hanging out there. There was, but he was all dressed up and declined to officiate on my slimy sack of eels. He said, anyway, they were too stiff to do anything with just then.

A woman who came in and heard me asking questions about eel skinning asked me why I bothered. She said, in her family, they simply cut them up unskinned and fried them. Then, when you ate them, you avoided the skin.

Someone else urged me to see the shellfish warden about eel skinning. I was told he was an old pro.

I found him busy sawing beams in his carpenter's shop, but he readily agreed to be of help. He said he would warm up my sackful of eels in front of his electric heater, and once they were defrosted, do the skinning.

An hour later, when I returned, there they were, skinless and neat, laid out on waxed paper—a far cry from the slimy, rigid loops of earlier. They really did look delectable enough to eat, so I asked what was the best way to cook them.

Stifle, I was told, was, of course, delicious. It is a Vineyard specialty, I learned—eels "stifled" in potatoes, salt pork and onions, or I could simply cut them up and fry them in a little fat. I said I'd heard they jumped around in the pan like Mexican jumping beans when you did that. The shellfish warden chuckled. He said he thought mine were dead enough to keep still in the pan, and wished me luck and sent me off.

Black Revolution

Julius Lester is a newcomer to Gay Head, who talks softly of the Vineyard as "the enchanted island." He is also an angry young writer who is called the literary spokesman for the black revolution.

He stubbed out cigarettes in a scallop shell the other day at the house that he has rented for the winter overlooking Vineyard Sound, and talked of black revolution and black writers, and an America of the future.

Outside, snow was falling in big, wet flakes that made doily patterns as they drifted past the window.

"Is there going to be a black revolution? There already has been in consciousness," Mr. Lester said. "There's been a total transformation in recent years in how black people view themselves and everything around them. The whole Black Studies thing is an example of it. Every Monday I fly to New York to teach a course in black history at the New School for Social Research, and I have my own radio program, 'The Great Proletarian Cultural Revolution,' essentially aimed at the black community, on WBAI. You didn't have things like that a few years ago.

"And now, at last, racism has become a part of the American vocabulary. It never was before. People talked about prejudice and discrimination, but they didn't talk about racism. A healthy confrontation with whites has been forced. But what's in the future? That's something we still can't know. White attitudes and consciousness have to change or there's going to be a physical confrontation that could bring about the destruction of the country."

Mr. Lester opened a Coca Cola. He is a slender, bespectacled young man with a Vandyke beard.

"It looks very pessimistic as far as Middle America—the solid white majority—is concerned," he said. "On the other hand, if you take hippies, the radicals—a good part of the young—then you have a different kind of consciousness. The question is, do these young people of the future have a chance to become the present before it's too late? Among other things, I'm made very pessimistic by the present administration—it's very popular with the people in Ohio and Indiana and all those other weird places we snobs on the East Coast don't think about. Not until Wallace and Agnew and the present day did you have spokesmen for militant white thought, even if you had militant whites, and this frightens me."

Mr. Lester went to the cupboard for a bag of potato chips. Munching them, he continued.

"It isn't just the blacks who have a problem in this

country," he said. "The guilt rests with a certain way we have of doing things here.

"You shouldn't have to have an inquest into whether two Black Panthers were shot by the police. You'll end up, of course, with a certain number of cops blamed and used as scapegoats, but man, who sent those cops over there in the first place? That's the question.

"To prevent a militant black revolution, there's going to have to be an all-out revolution in American society—not just in consciousness, but in economic and social institutions. There's going to have to be a revolution not just in terms of greater equality, but you're going to have to start educating people to be decent human beings, not just to get jobs.

"You're going to have to see to it that men aren't condemned to work in a paper-box factory for life. That's soul-destroying. And it's just ridiculous, you know, that people should be poor when there's enough in this country for all.

"Our attitude now is, 'OK, you're poor. That's because you don't work.' I say a man's life isn't just working to earn money for food and nothing else. There'll never be a solution of black problems in this country until everything else is changed, too—until in a city like New York, people aren't living in an apartment with rats and that whole scene."

Mr. Lester's eyes wandered toward the window, where peaceful woodland stretched. His train of thought changed. "I can't pinpoint it," he said, "but there's something that makes this Island a very, very special place—a place where I think I'd like my children to grow up and go to school. You just can't do that properly in New York City anymore."

A native of Nashville, Tennessee, Julius Lester moved to New York in 1961. By then, he had been graduated from Fiske University and had made up his mind that he wanted to be a writer (although he is also a photographer, folk singer and guitarist who has made several recordings).

"What could I do in Nashville? Be a school teacher? Work in the Ford plant? Be a janitor in the post office?"

So he headed for New York, taking jobs with the Welfare Department, in bookstores and camps while he wrote, giving some folk-singing concerts and teaching guitar. He became an editor of *Sing Out* magazine, and then joined SNCC—the Student Nonviolent Coordinating Committee. He was its photographer when Stokely Carmichael was its chairman. He stayed with it until 1968.

"Stokely today? He's in Conakry, Guinea, as Nkrumah's personal secretary. He's been working to get Nkrumah back into power as president of Ghana and make it a center for black power. I'm pretty skeptical about the likelihood of that, though. If the Ghanaians were saying it, that would be one thing—but this way. . .?"

Except for his black history class and his radio program, all of Mr. Lester's time nowadays is taken up with his writing. In the last year and a half, he has produced five books and more than a dozen articles. He finds the "live and let live" quality of the Vineyard, he said, exceptionally good for writing.

"I don't feel any hostile pressures here at all. If you want to be left alone, people will leave you alone." But he grinned. "Everyone will end up knowing your business anyway."

At present, he is at work on a book of short stories and a piece comparing the politics of Eldridge Cleaver with those of Stokely Carmichael.

"I would say that I find a lot of things Stokely says more relevant than what Cleaver says. We both think racism is the major problem, not capitalism. As far as Cleaver is concerned, I think he's set things back in terms of making premature alliances with white radicals, and then in the way he's said white capitalism is the more important thing to be fought, and in his irresponsible use of the rhetoric of violence. The black writer, Chester Himes, you know, has described unorganized violence as 'like a blind man with a pistol,' and I think that's right."

Mr. Lester writes his articles quickly, but rewrites extensively. "I never really remember how many articles I have to do at one time. I just have a list with the deadline dates beside them. But you see, I've been miraculously lucky in my life. The first book I wrote, I did when a publisher asked me to. When it didn't end up with black and white going off into the sunset hand in hand, he wouldn't buy it, but I met an agent who was interested, and the first publisher he took it to bought it. That was *Look Out, Whitey, Black Power's Gon' Get Your Mama.* After that, assignments and ideas just kept coming my way."

Mr. Lester's other books include *To Be a Slave*, the 1969 runner-up for the Newbery Medal for outstanding writing for children, *Search for the New Land* and *Revolutionary Notes*. He has just completed an anthology of the writings of the black economist, W.E.B. DuBois, started in June in Gay Head, and finished last month.

Although he, himself, is more a prose than a poetry writer, it is poetry, he feels, that is the major medium of black expression in the literary arts at the moment.

"It's more accessible than prose. To read Western fiction today—to read anyone but Jacqueline Susann, anyway—you have to have training. To understand Nabokov, you need to be literate in five languages. To read Vonnegut, there's a special art. We need a black form of fiction that wouldn't require all that training to understand. But we don't have it yet, though I think the '70's may see it. But while we're waiting, we do have poetry.

"Black poetry is quite a thing nowadays. It's close to the old tradition. You can get up in front of an audience and read a poem—in coffee houses, bookstores, on campuses—all over the black community you have poetry readings. Black poets realize their model for a poem can't be something like Keats or Shelley or Yeats. It should communicate in the same sense that the songs of soul singers like James Brown and Aretha Franklin do. Don L. Lee is one of the good poets. So is Larry Neal. There are a couple of black companies now that are publishing nothing but poetry and it's selling very well."

LeRoi Jones, according to Mr. Lester, remains a leading black literary influence. "He's a good writer. He's even achieved popularity in the white community, but he turned his back on it. He became a sort of a model for black men—politically and culturally. As far as Baldwin is concerned, I think he's been killed by fame. It's a vicious thing. A writer's job is not to be on the cover of *Time*. Ralph Ellison? He's sort of fallen into disrepute. He hasn't done anything in a long time. That doesn't mean he's not going to.

"What I think we need is some fiction dealing with the protest movement and the peace movement. We have umpteen nonfiction books about protest, but no fiction, and there's no other medium that can do the things fiction can do. There's just no substitute for a *The Brothers Karamazov*. You can't get inside a character with nonfiction, or even with a film, the way you can with fiction. As far as I'm concerned, I fell into nonfiction accidentally, and hope to get out of it."

Then Mr. Lester began to watch the snow disappearing into the woods, and he talked of Gay Head and the Island's Indians whose home it is; who scallop when the weather is right, loaf when it isn't, and feud together with relish.

"There are problems here," he said, "but there's something that makes this Island a very, very special place."

Sunsets
and
Sea Mosses

In winter, there is only one householder on Chappaquiddick's west side, and she is diminutive and white-haired and eighty-seven. She lives alone with her dog, watching the sunsets and the sea mosses and the moods of the bay—its gray-green turbulence on storm days, its sparkling blueness under a February sun.

She burns wood in a pot-bellied stove, and has used three cords so far this winter. Despite arthritis that has gnarled her hands and slowed the stride that was always called in Edgartown her "Chappaquiddick gait," Georgie Thomas still gathers her own wood from her woodpile, scrubs her kitchen and parlor floors every morning, and with Yankee self-sufficiency firmly declines all offers of aid and all suggestions that, now that she is almost a nonagenarian, it might be wiser if she would move into Edgartown.

"It's quiet, and I like being by the water," is the way she put it last week when I dropped by. "In Edgartown, they don't like dogs in houses, and I don't want to go out in the backwoods. I used to live over in Edgartown, of course. I had seventeen babies born at my house there when I was nursing. But I love it here, though I'm afraid I won't be able to stay another year. It's getting harder to get the wood into the stove, and I haven't my car anymore. When I had it, I'd drive down into town quite often, but now I only get my mail once a week and the Jeffers girls bring my groceries. But I don't want to go. That's all there is to it!" And she opened the stove grate to add another handful of kindling, and prepared instant coffee from the kettle that always steams on the stove top. She moves stiffly because of the arthritis, but it never keeps her from moving. Her affliction maddens her, but she makes sure it does not stop her.

"Excuse me," she says of her slowness. "I'm only twenty-five, you know, but I walk like a woman of 125."

"Oh, if coffee was intoxicating, I'd be drunk now," she continued. "There's so much already there, you can hear it splash when it goes down." And she settled down with her cup at her work table, where, for decades, she has designed sea moss greeting cards and painstakingly attached miniature scallop shells to matchbook covers.

"I wish the mosses were better nowadays," she said cryptically, opening a box of her handiwork. "Last summer, there were no nice ones at all coming in, though I wasn't able to walk the beach very much anyway. I used to be quite a walker when I was a youngster. I'd walk down to Wasque all the time. Usually I'd take the road because, if you take the beach, there's one creek you have to cross and another you have to wade across or go way up and around, but I'd do my moss and shell hunting on the beach, of course. I certainly need some decent shells right now, too," she said. "They've been as bad lately as the moss.

"Yesterday, before the harbor froze over, though, you should have seen the mosses. It looked as if we were getting the good ones back again. I don't know what the quality close up was, but from a distance, it was just like a green field out there. If I could have, I would have gone out and collected some. I separate the strands with a little round toothpick, once I've got a good supply, and then I dry them on the porch.

"Yesterday reminded me," Mrs. Thomas said, and her eyes sparkled mischievously from behind her harlequin glasses, "as I was looking out at those mosses, of Prohibition days. There was a boat a little way off South Beach, I noticed, just waiting there, and I remembered how, in Prohibition, there would always be boats out there, and the fishermen would go out and buy their liquor. We lived out here on Chappy one year during Prohibition. That was about all I managed, though, when my husband was alive. He came from Maine and he didn't like it a bit over here. He always liked a lot of people around, so we were in Edgartown mostly.

"Freckles," Mrs. Thomas interrupted to talk to her furry, brown dog. "It's time you went out," and she led her toward the door.

Georgie Thomas was born Georgianna Ripley Sandsbury "in a cluster of houses by the narrowest part of Chappaquiddick.

"And I have a twin brother, Oscar," she explained, "who lives in Rhode Island now. He used to be a captain of the steamship line, though he never learned to swim. I said to him once, 'Now, Oscar, don't you wish you'd learned how to swim?' And he said to me, 'What good would it do me in the middle of Nantucket Sound?' And I guess he was right. It never did matter. He's survived to be a great-grandfather now.

"You know, the other day, some men came here with gas for the heater in the kitchen, and they were curious about me living here all alone, and they asked how old I was. 'Oh, I have a license to drive a car,' I told them, 'and I can vote,' " and she chuckled at the recollection.

Only the most perceptive, seeing Georgie Thomas in a green sweater, black slacks and blue sneakers, with her fingernails carefully manicured, would have any idea that she was eighty-seven. Perhaps her youthful appearance stems from the many years she swam, winter as well as summer, in Katama Bay.

"Mrs. May West—a friend of mine, not *the* Mae West—and I used to go swimming from Osborn's Pier by the ferry," she said. "We did it all winter, though when there was ice floating around the ferry that did bother us a little. You felt as if the ice were chasing you. That was the trouble!"

In the time when Georgie Thomas was born on Chappaquiddick, and was a child growing up, a good many more people lived on the Island than today, she recalled. "The white people lived on this side, and the Indians on the other. People were mostly fishermen or farmers. I remember there was one Indian who drove oxen. He used to deliver ice, and there was a hill down in back of our house, and he'd always give me a ride. Then my father made me stop asking him because he said the hill was too steep, and I was giving Mr. Belain too much trouble. William Belain, he was.

"Freckles, go chase a bird," Mrs. Thomas called to her barking dog through the window. "Stop making so much noise." But when the barking did not cease, sighing, Mrs. Thomas went to let her in.

"How did we happen to live over here when I was little? I guess it was because, in the summer, my father used to take parties fishing and sailing, and this was a good place to be for that, and my mother took in boarders. And in the winter, this was a good place to dig clams. But when I was ten years old, we moved to Edgartown. I guess it was easier when I was in school. Otherwise, my father always had to row me over, or if it was cold enough, I could go on the ice. The ferry didn't run so much then. The ferry in those days was a rowboat, and Charles Osborn was the ferryman. He was blind, but he knew the way back and forth absolutely by heart."

Mrs. Thomas refilled her coffee mug, set it between a *Yankee* magazine and a bottle of hand lotion, and, now that recollections were spinning, recounted to me how she had happened to get her name.

"Of course, my mother knew a baby was going to be born, so she sent my father into Edgartown after the doctor. On the way, because he was afraid he might not get back in time, he asked a neighbor, Mrs. Ripley, if she would stay with my mother. Sure enough, no sooner had my father left than my brother, Oscar, was born, and then there I was, unexpectedly. Of course, my mother was grateful to Mrs. Ripley and she wanted to pay her something, but Mrs. Ripley said she wouldn't think of accepting money. 'Then, instead,' said my mother, 'you name the girl anything you like.' And that's how I became Georgianna Ripley Sandsbury. But don't you dare call me anything but Georgie or I'll sic the dog on you!" Whereupon Freckles turned her brown and white freckled nose happily toward her mistress and leaped responsively.

Now that she gets out very little, Georgie Thomas finds that she goes to bed early. "After the six o'clock news, usually. I might just as well in the wintertime, anyway. It gets dark at four. But I'm always up before seven. I used to read a great deal, but my eyes aren't so good for it now, and then I used to go down at extreme low tide to dig clams in front of the house, but I guess my clamming days are over," she sighed.

A nurse for many years, Mrs. Thomas reminisces happily about the days when she worked with Dr. Orland Mayhew and Dr. Charles F. Lane and Dr. Channing Nevin. Much of her work was home nursing that took her to all parts of the Island.

"Especially in the summer there were always plenty of people who needed help, and some who didn't, but thought they should have it," she commented in her no-nonsense way.

"Now, look, look," she said, peering beyond a poinsettia by her window, and looking down Katama Bay. "Just take a look at the way it is here when the sun is going down, and it's so pinkish on the fields. Can you blame me for liking it? I wish there were a little grocery store here, but that's all I miss. Once, there was a Mr. Handy here who would take orders, and had kept some flour and sugar and canned goods outside his house, and that was nice, but it's the closest to a store Chappaquiddick ever has had, as far as I know. Over in the field, those Jeffers girls had a restaurant for a while, and they served the most marvelous meals, and once there was a trailer that served meals down on the South Shore, but we haven't had much else in the way of businesses. We had a church, of course, but it was blown down in a hurricane. The ministers would take turns and come over from Edgartown. I wish they'd start a church over here again."

The fire needed to be fed again. She warmed her hands by it, and its blazing put her in mind of the day her husband, a professional fisherman, caught a thirty-two-pound lobster.

"He brought it home, and I took one look at it and I said, 'My heavens, I'm not going to cook anything as big as that.' But he said I needn't worry about it, he'd take care of it. So he split it underneath and filled it with buttered breadcrumbs and broiled it over charcoal in the fireplace, and I've never had anything so good in my life.

"What sort of fishing did my husband do? All sorts. He had his own boat that he named for me. You couldn't blame the poor boat. Soon as it had my name, it gave out!

"Well now, let me see if I can think of a couple of other things to tell you about what I used to do here when I was more active. I used to dig up old, rusty anchors, for example. Don't ask me why, but they came in handy after one of the hurricanes when boats were washed up all along the shore here. Yes, certainly, I've been here in a hurricane. I sat on my porch and watched a wave getting bigger and bigger, and I thought 'That's it for my porch. I guess I'd better go inside.' And then, all of a sudden, the wave just went away.

"Now come out and let me show you the porch," she said, "and everything I can see from it." And she rose slowly and stepped out into the brisk dusk air.

"Lots of times, I sit out on the porch for hours and watch the water, and when it gets dark I watch the lights go on, one by one, across Katama Bay. I like it best on clear days, but it's exciting in a storm, too. Oh, how that ocean roars!

"Well, now, you must come over this summer sometime and I'll drag you down to the beach and we can look for moss."

Then Georgie Thomas bade me good-bye, waving from the back porch of her big, weathered, shingle house. As I turned to drive away, I noticed she was shaking off the doormat and beginning to sweep—arthritis notwithstanding—with the vigor of a forty year old.

Oiled
Birds

Each beach that I have walked today has been a sticky graveyard. I am reminded of Uncle Remus' Tar Baby.

The sands are dotted with oil-stiffened birds. In the waves near shore those that are not yet dead flap helplessly, seeking to wash the hardening blackness from their bellies and wings. There was a loon near the high tide mark—I recognized it, though I had only seen one before, by its long beak. They are not uncommon here, but neither are they an everyday sort of bird. The one I saw before was on Thanksgiving Day at Menemsha, disappearing at one end of the bight, shaking its head, cocking it a little to one side before deep-diving again after another tasty holiday morsel. It was all alone on the bight except for a duck, a handful of gulls and one scallop fisherman, dredging, I supposed, for a first course for Thanksgiving dinner.

The loon seemed to be having such a lovely time of it. There was a smugness in its demeanor that made me laugh.

But this morning there was only a wretched, sticky creature in the sand, fluttering when it could gather the strength to flutter, wings and body coated with sand as well as with thick black oil, bright eyes trembling.

The Coast Guard and Natural Resource officers have been scouring the beaches, seeking those least severely damaged in hopes that a few of the more than eight hundred murres, cormorants, razor-billed auks, eider ducks, gulls and mergansers that are thrashing along the Island's South Shore from Gay Head to Wasque, and in the tall grasses of the great ponds, can be saved. No one is certain quite how to do it. Detergents destroy the natural oil that keeps the birds insulated against the cold, I am told, but M.S.P.C.A. officials will try all the same. Youngsters by the hundreds have been called out to help in the bathing.

No one knows where the oil has come from. Coast Guard helicopters sent to see if they could locate a slick have reported back that they find nothing, except a thick area of algae. Perhaps, they are proposing, it is this and not oil that is affecting the birds. But the coastguardsmen on the beaches know better. Sand is coagulated. Fist-sized black gobs bob near the shore. Beach grass is matted and worn down where birds have sought to scrape themselves clean. At Squibnocket, the blackened rocks have a volcanic look.

The Scrubby Neck beach, from a distance, looks seaweed-strewn, but then, as one draws closer, it is clear that the dark patches are neither brown sea moss nor skate egg cases nor rockweed.

The owners of that beach have tried to rake the oil clumps

together and are burning them, with tarred driftwood and pathetic bird corpses.

Many of the birds, if they survive the oil itself, are expected to die from respiratory infections contracted as they have flapped in the sand. And the sea ducks have a special problem. Though they may be rescued and bathed, if they stay on dry land to recover, their feet will dry and crack painfully unless they are treated with a lubricating ointment. Then there is the question of food. The laughable, penguin-like murres, the auks, the scoters—all eat live food, and it is thought unlikely that, in captivity, they will be willing to eat anything else.

Many of the rescues have been touching, but it seems so sad that there need be rescues at all. One of the coast-guardsmen I met at South Beach told of a boy he had seen at Quenames who went, fully clad, chest-deep into the icy water after a mute swan. And there was an elderly lady with a basket and a blanket whom they told me of, seeking a bird to save.

This is such a clear, bright Sunday. The sun is sparkling on snow patches. We have had weekend guests, and yesterday, before the stricken birds had begun to wash ashore, we walked along Katama. The children in our party raced the beach, collecting driftwood, pebbles, burnished stones and sea-smooth glass to take back to the city "to make it like the lovely country," one of them said.

Today, their parents prefer that they be kept away from the ugly beach.

A Visit
With the
Sage of
West Tisbury

February 11

On a wintry evening, there is no cosier place to be in West Tisbury than by the oil stove at Joseph E. Howes' when the tin of gingersnaps is out, and Mr. Howes—the sage of West Tisbury—is talking of brigs and whaleships, or of home-steading and panning for gold in the Far West, and dodging bullets in the Pancho Villa uprising.

Yesterday, I went to see him in his plum-colored living room with the window cactuses in bloom, town reports of the last half-century scattered on the Victorian sofa, and Dr. Charles E. Banks' *History of Martha's Vineyard* always near at hand.

Joe Howes is ninety-six, but until last year, he was still town inspector of animals, of milk and of slaughtering. Then he found that a mile was about as far as he could walk without getting tired, and since he was in the habit of walking from farm to farm, he felt obliged to resign his posts. "But I expect I'm the only man in the state who was holding down three town offices at ninety-five," he says proudly.

His age notwithstanding, Joe Howes remains hardy–bent only a trifle from the six-foot height of his youth. He is across the road at Alley's General Store each noon when mail is distributed, adding a bright touch to the decor of hardware and grocery boxes in his red-and-black-checked flannel shirt, pants held in place by yellow and red calico galluses. At one o'clock, he is still likely to be in the store, earnestly arguing about local politics. When I knocked at his door about sunset yesterday, he had just come in from feeding his horse.

I told him I had come to him in his capacity as sage of West Tisbury, for some of his recollections of Island history.

He rubbed the top of his bald head thoughtfully.

"Well," he said, as soon as he had settled down among pillows in his big chair by the back window, "I can tell you that the year 1892 was a very unusual year. It was very cold that winter. But that was before I came to the Vineyard. I lived across the way on the island of Naushon. I remember that we looked out one morning and we couldn't see anything but ice between Tarpaulin Cove and West Chop. It may have been that year, too, or else it was the late '80's, when there was that big water spout halfway between Nobska Point and Oak Bluffs. The sun was shining bright and nice as could be–I think it was in August–but some of the vessels coming over the shoals at that time, it nearly swamped them."

Mr. Howes took off his gold-rimmed glasses and examined them ruminatively.

"You know, in '88–I was twelve years old at the time:

that was when we moved from East Harwich to Naushon—it was no unusual thing to see sailing vessels lying in the cove at Tarpaulin. My brother was customs house officer at Naushon—that's how we happened to go there. There used to be a good many whalers and barks and brigs from everywhere that would come in, and he would have to examine their cargoes."

Mr. Howes chuckled, thinking back, at a tale or two of salvage.

"The Sound used to be full of barges and towboats, too, in those days, and they did a lot of wrecking. Every winter, there'd be two or three vessels ashore, and then the wreckers would come to get whatever they could. My brother used to try to get the wrecks for Captain Charlie Davis of New Bedford. But there was also Captain Harvey Cook who worked out of Vineyard Haven, and the two were in competition.

"I remember one time a vessel came in loaded with Turks Island salt and struck Humility Rock off Naushon. My brother went hurrying out there to see if he could get the job of taking care of the salt load for Captain Davis. He managed to get there before Captain Cook, and he told the captain of the salt vessel to be sure not to have anything to do with him, but to wait till Captain Davis arrived. The captain liked the looks of my brother, I guess, and he agreed.

"Well, Captain Davis got there and promised that within ten minutes of the time the contract was signed, he'd have the vessel's load lightened, and she'd be on her way to getting off the rock. Of course, the contract was signed right away. But as soon as it was signed, Captain Davis went away to New Bedford and didn't come back for two days. Meanwhile, Captain Cook had come and been sent away. You can imagine, the salt captain was fit to be tied. But when Captain

Davis came back, he said he'd kept his word, hadn't he? While he was away, the vessel had lightened, hadn't she? And he was right, of course. After all, the rock had made a hole in the bottom of the vessel, and in two days' time quite a lot of salt had poured out!

"Now there's another good story about the vessels of those days I think I'll tell you," Mr. Howes continued. "It was in 1887 that this one happened. A ship loaded with watermelons went ashore on Naushon. She had watermelons on her deck and flour and cheese in her hold. The quickest way to lighten that load, of course, was to throw the watermelons overboard, and for more than a week there were watermelons bobbing all over the Sound. Old Captain Bunker of Vineyard Haven saw good business in that, so he took his sloop and knocked off fishing for black bass, filled his boat up with watermelons, took them off to Newport and sold them for fifteen cents apiece. He even came back after a second load."

In Joe Howes' near century of living, he has had a multitude of occupations and adventures and savors recalling every one of them. He paused a moment to tend his oil stove and proffer ginger ale. Then he reminisced about how he had met five Presidents—Cleveland, Theodore Roosevelt, Coolidge, Wilson and McKinley. Cleveland and McKinley he remembers with particular warmth.

"I met Cleveland when I was about sixteen and he was on Naushon gunning. He was about six feet tall and weighed 350 pounds, I expect. As for me, in those days I was all arms and legs. I was asked to carry his gun and his coat down to his station for him—that was where he was shooting deer—and I put his coat on because that was the easiest way to carry it. Then, all of a sudden, there he was coming up the path. I was embarrassed, of course, but he just smiled at me and said, 'Boy, if it fitted you any better, I'd give it to you.' Fancy,"

Joe Howes said, "getting that close to a President nowadays."

It was at the Buffalo Exposition, the day before McKinley was shot, that Mr. Howes had his encounter with him. Joe Howes was there on a tour with the New England Grocers' Association. The President talked to him at some length of the Vineyard, he remembers, and peppered him with questions. He talked of being interested in paying the Island a visit sometime. "The next day, on the way home, I heard he'd been shot in the Hall of Music," Mr. Howes said.

"I met Teddy Roosevelt," he continued, "when he came into a store I was running in North Falmouth once. Let me show you the handkerchief he gave me," and Mr. Howes reached into the voluminous chest of drawers by his television set where he keeps memorabilia and notes to himself of historic happenings on scraps of envelopes and ends of paper, and pulled out a red and white kerchief decorated with T.R.'s and Rough Rider hats.

"This dates from the second time that he ran for President," Mr. Howes said. "He was with the Bull Moose party then, and he came into the store with General Leonard Wood, who'd been head of the Philippines and had a house in Pocasset. He gave me a dozen of these kerchiefs to help get a few votes from the farmers, don't you know. Oh, he was a big man, too—six feet tall, anyway, and he had a heavy moustache. 'He was Teddy Rough and Ready. Be a Rabbit. Get the Habit. Increase and Multiply.' That was the jingle about him.

"It was while I was in North Falmouth, too, that I met Calvin Coolidge. They called him 'Cross-No-Word-Puzzle.' I was a delegate for him when he was running for governor of Massachusetts. Three years after that, I guess it was, I was in the waiting room in the railroad station one day, and this man was sitting there reading a magazine, and he got up and said, 'Mr. Howes, I'm Mr. Coolidge; you were one of my delegates, and I'm pleased to meet you.' And I was very much pleased, too, because there were quite a few delegates.

"As for Wilson, he was visiting his son and daughter-in-law right here on the Island, on West Chop—that was where I saw him. He was very prim.

"I expect you want to know, though, how it happened that I got from Naushon to Martha's Vineyard, and forget all the other nonsense."

He snapped his suspenders jauntily and recollected that his first visit to the Island had been in 1892, for a masquerade ball.

"I bought me a pair of patent leathers for the occasion," he remembered. "The dance was in Vineyard Haven, where the town hall is now, and when I got ready to come out of that dance, the snow had come so fast it was a regular smotherer. I think it must have been two feet deep, and it was still coming down so fast I couldn't see a single, solitary thing. I was staying at Captain Vincent's on Main Street, and it took me quite some time to find my way back. In those days, they just had those little square oil lanterns to light your way. When I finally got there, Mrs. Vincent—she was one of those good old souls— said, 'Well, we knew you'd be soaked, but not *that* soaked. You go into your room and pass out all the clothes that are wet and I'll dry them for you by morning, though I don't know what we can do about your patent leathers.'

"There just wasn't much that could be done. By morning, they were like two herrings, and my pants were shrunk so I could hardly wear them. She had to lend me the captain's boots to wear down to the wharf."

It was two years later, however, before Joe Howes took a job on the Vineyard. By then, the Naushon customs house had been closed because fewer and fewer vessels were stopping there, and the whole Howes family moved to the Island. Among his yellowed papers, Mr. Howes still has the letter from Mrs. P. Moller of Vineyard Haven that offered him "$25 a month but no room" for working at her West Chop estate.

"So I took the job and drove her horse and a fancy wagon for her. It was in the days of electric cars, and she needed a man with a firm hand on the reins," Mr. Howes recalled, "for she had a horse that was afraid of trains. So, in the afternoons, I'd put on my light trousers and my kid gloves and my cutaway and my stiff derby hat and my black tie and I'd take the family over to Oak Bluffs."

That same year, Mr. Howes remembers with a sparkle in his gray-blue eyes, he took a part-time job one day driving the hearse from Vineyard Haven to the Chilmark cemetery.

"I was still new to the Island, and I didn't know where the cemetery was, but I expected I'd be able to find it. I was told all I had to do was follow the carriage with the pallbearers. They told me there'd be four of them in a covered wagon, and that I'd meet them at the junction of William Street and the State Road.

"I got to the foot of William Street all right, and I waited and waited, and after a while along came a covered wagon with curtains and I began to follow it. The driver turned off on the Lambert's Cove Road, so I turned off, too. Pretty soon, the wagon turned off toward Makonikey. Even though I was new, I thought that was a pretty strange way to get to Chilmark. Well, finally I was sure I was going the wrong way, and wondered how I'd ever catch up with the funeral party, but I kept on going with the remains. I got as far as the Methodist Church and there began to be an awful odor. 'Uh-oh,' I thought, 'this is a hot day and I've been driving too long, and something's happened to the remains.' It was just about then I met old Deacon Pease. I told him where I was going, and he said, of course, I was on the wrong track, and gave me directions back, and then I asked him about the smell. 'It doesn't come from here, does it?' I asked, nodding toward the remains and feeling nervous about asking.

" 'Why, of course not,' he said, and he laughed and he laughed. 'That smell comes from William Look's pig sty.' After that, I hustled right back to the main road and there the whole procession was looking for me. I got back about five that night and I'd made $1. Maybe it wasn't much, but it was twenty-five cents more than it would have been if I'd just worked on the road that day. That was the other job I was doing, and it only paid fifteen cents an hour."

From road work, carriage driving and leading funeral corteges, Mr. Howes moved on to manage his own laundry and then to go to work as a grocery clerk.

"I used to ride a bicycle with kerosene cans and molasses jugs. That job was with the Look, Washburn Produce Company in Vineyard Haven, but there were too many temptations to spend money in Vineyard Haven and I decided to move to West Tisbury. You got more money there, anyway, for clerking."

Then there came the time when Joe Howes thought he would like to see the Pacific Ocean, so he strapped $2,500 in savings around his waist and set off for the West. For two years, he traveled from Alaska to Mexico.

"I'd get on the good side of the railway brakemen. I'd tell them I was hard up. You had to play hard up or they'd knock you in the head. And maybe I'd help out a little with freight and I'd get a free ride that way. I never spent a dollar when I could make a dollar.

"Those were the days when the Western Pacific had just

started and they were having homeseekers' excursions. They'd give you 160 acres of land if you'd guarantee to stay and work it for three years. I went out to Nevada on one of those trips, but then I learned that in the Sierra Nevadas sometimes you had as much as thirty feet of snow, and I didn't like that idea, so I decided I'd see if I could pan for gold instead. But when I didn't strike any gold, I gave that up pretty soon, too, and got myself a job in the Emporium in San Francisco selling men's stockings.

"It was dull work, but that was one thing I could do—selling—and I got $25 or $30 a week. For a while after that I worked in the toy department, and then they gave me a job lacing corsets, and that was the last of my jobs there. The Barbary queens were too much for me!"

Briefly, in Tijuana, Mr. Howes thought of going into business in a general store, but a letter from his sister-in-law told him that his brother was ill and hoped he would come to help him in his Vineyard Haven drygoods store.

"I hated to let that Mexican store go by," Mr. Howes said, and sighed mightily, "but there wasn't very much I could do about it, so I started back. The first place I stopped was Juarez, and if you turn around you'll see a serape I bought there right behind you on that settee," and Mr. Howes nodded toward the still vividly red garment flung across his Victorian sofa, below two Winslow Homer prints of sailing ships.

"The day I mailed that was quite a day," he reminisced. "I got to the post office with the serape at 3 P.M. and at 5 P.M. the bullets were zipping in El Paso. It was the start of the Pancho Villa uprising. I got out just in time."

Back on the Vineyard, he tried his hand only briefly at his brother's store. Then, on doctor's orders that he work outdoors, he bought land at Tea Lane for a cranberry bog.

That same year, 1914, he married the West Tisbury schoolteacher, Bessie C. Howes ("She changed her name, but not the letter, for the worse, not the better," he rhymes, though adding, of course, that it is not quite accurate), remodeled a house at Tea Lane to go with his 180 acres, and built a henhouse.

"I bought 350 hens and chickens and thought I'd go into the poultry business along with the cranberries, but that was the year—the only year— that the roup ever hit the Island, and it killed half my birds.

"Those weren't very good times for me in any respect. The next year, although my cranberry bog was bearing in good shape, the war was in full swing and the price for cranberries dropped from $12 a barrel to $3, and since it cost $4 a barrel to pick, screen and ship them, that would have put me in debt if I'd kept on picking them, so I said to myself, 'I'll raise vegetables instead. Truck farming will be good.' But it wasn't. On account of the war, you couldn't hire anyone to help.

"Well, I started in anyway. I started my garden early, but the first week in June came a hard frost and killed all my potatoes. And the fourth year of those bad years, the armyworms struck. They're about an inch long and kind of gray and destroy crops. The whole earth was moving with them. The armyworm and the locust struck the same year, and that was one of the worst ones.

"But the fifth year was absolutely the worst of all. I decided I'd try the milk business if nothing else would work, and I bought fifteen head of cattle from Noman's Land. But that was the year the Massachusetts cattle inspectors came down here and found a lot of cattle with TB. They carried them off-Island by the truckload. And that was the end of my dairy. The only good thing that happened in all that time was that my wife decided she'd have a baby."

By 1918, Mr. Howes had had more than his fill of farming, and when he read that the government was seeking people to take the farm census on the Island, it sounded like a tempting job possibility.

"It was August, I remember, and it was hotter than Tophet when I went to take the exams. I came home and I said to my wife, 'I guess I didn't pass.' But then, about the middle of December when there was crusted snow about eighteen inches deep, I got word that I'd been appointed enumerator, not just for Chilmark, here on the Island, but for Noman's Land and the Elizabeth Islands, as well. And they wanted to know, too, if I'd help out in West Tisbury. I spent that whole month walking in snow fifteen to eighteen inches deep."

Since neither farming nor census taking proved half so appealing as Mr. Howes had dreamed, he decided to go back to storekeeping, but the doctor was still urging him to stay out of doors, so he bought a truck and some drygoods, candy, cigarettes, tonic and groceries, and began going from door to door with them.

"And that was the business I kept on with till the truck burned up in a fire in my barn sixteen years ago. I bought another car afterwards, and I kept a good trade going for about two winters. But by then I was eighty-two years old, so I retired. I just kept my little garden. I had five thousand gladiolas and four hundred strawberry plants. I used to sell my gladiolas for $1 a dozen. I guess it was six years ago I stopped that. My equilibrium wasn't what it used to be."

Mr. Howes paused. He said he thought he had "talked enough slush" and it was time for more ginger ale and to break out the gingersnaps.

"Folks think they work hard now," he said, as he dived into the gingersnaps.

Spring
Signs

Today is spring, and I have been in search of its signs.

I have seen three red-winged blackbirds. Although I am not yet countrified enough to know immediately that they mean spring, I am told that they do—that their shrill whistle is a sure sign that warm days lie ahead. Last night a pattern of Canada geese flew over West Tisbury on their way north.

There are still a few snowbirds—juncos—feeding at Vineyard Haven feeders, but they are being made to feel definitely out of place.

In the woods, moss is a chartreuse shade nowadays. It is thicker and more effulgent than when I last looked at it at the edge of a rock after a midwinter snow.

Everywhere, color and light seem to be different. A softness is beginning to come in the air. The clean blue sky of winter and fall is baby blue now. Hills that were brown begin to be lavender and pink. Spring is a pastel season.

I have been looking for crocuses, and was cross till this morning because I could find none. Then I was told to stop at Mrs. Mabel Johnson's dooryard on the Edgartown-West Tisbury Road to see the snowdrops, and a yellow crocus and a purple one were sprouting. When I knelt to cup a fragile snowdrop in my hand, the earth cushioned my knee, and there, I knew, was another sign of spring.

Mrs. Johnson's snowdrops are everywhere in West Tisbury, I am told—given in little parcels through the years to lighten winter-weary hearts, for they nod so prettily so early in the spring. Indeed, this year at least, they have preceded the season's official arrival.

The daffodils are up, a wag tells me, outside at least one town hall, "Because of all the hot air," he avers. Unfortunately, whenever I visit the town hall I am hurrying too fast to look. One should never be hurrying that fast on the Vineyard. There is too much to be missed.

I saw some dark green teaberry leaves in the woods and grew excited, and wondered if they were a harbinger of the new season. I was afraid they were not. The deep green of their leaves inclined me to think that they were an evergreen, and I was right. But at least now, with snow gone and leaves matted down by rain, they can be seen.

The arbutus must be under the leaves, too, in warm places—if I can discover where the warm places are. I am told they grow well in the fire lanes and along the sides of the road, and that I will find their tiny pink and white blossoms if I search patiently enough.

The speckled tents of the skunk cabbage should soon be up in dank places.

Last week at Menemsha, someone told me there were signs that might mean the herring were coming. But at the Chilmark Herring Creek on Sunday, there was only a black dog, and a clamdigger with a pitchfork and a ready smile. Although people start talking of herring in March, Everett H. Poole says it is sometimes not until May that they finally arrive. Menemsha Creek, though, is where they will make their first appearance, running up it some rainy or humid night before they head for the brooks to tumble against the tide and spawn.

Although there were no herring, there were carcasses and jawbones aplenty at the Herring Creek, to suggest that the ferocity of winter, and of man's winter pastimes, had taken their toll. A shark's jaw with its neat rim of scissor-sharp teeth was a memento of stormy seas battering sharks and shore. Red and green shotgun cartridges beside a dead loon and the stiff corpse of a duck gave witness to the sport of man when he is bored. The duck was an edible one, but its killer obviously had not shot for food. He had probably shot on a gray, chill Sunday afternoon when he could think of nothing more creative to do than kill.

On the Gay Head beach, I could find no spring signs, but I expect a beach is a poor place to go looking for them. Beaches, like mountains above the timber line, are eternal and largely unchanging aspects of the landscape—at least they are to me—though those who are more observant say that sands are gray in winter, but golden once spring comes. All that I notice is that there are more rocks on a beach when there are no swimmers to take them away.

And there were two barrels and a cable spool still undiscovered at noon Sunday—unheard-of treasures by that hour on a midsummer Sunday. But there was nothing that said "Spring! Spring!" to me as I walked, the way robins and flirtatious jonquils bobbing in a breeze do. The blond rocks were turning copper colored when they were wave-washed, and milky-white pebbles were scattered like pearls. But these, as I say, are everlasting. They are not indications of spring.

I have learned, though, that kids and lambs have begun to be born—a sure signal that the most hopeful of seasons is just around the corner. Everett Whiting has seven lambs.

When I went after the clothes on the line yesterday, they were not frozen to it in awkward shapes. I have had an encounter with a skunk, and although I realize we might have met face to face at any time of year, somehow it seems appropriate that our meeting was postponed till just about spring.

I expect to be seeing fat, shiny muskrats soon, and the mice in our walls scampered and scratched so last night that there could be no question but that they are in the first throes of spring fever. Reading to learn about rabbits at this time of year, I discovered that "mad as a March hare" refers to the male European hare's tumbling, leaping and fighting preparatory to spring mating.

A mud dauber (dormant wasp, I am told) was snoozing fitfully in our shed over the weekend. Several times, the sun warmed him enough so he awoke. He is getting ready, I expect, to start his wings whirring full force. I am beginning to be fearful of walking in the deep grass. There is no sign of poison ivy leaves yet, but it seems to me it must be about time for snakes to start uncoiling, and I have been wondering when it is that they form that grotesque writhing ball that one reads of unwinding, snake by snake, in the spring. Being something of a newcomer to the Vineyard, I am a trifle nervous about such things. Do Vineyard snakes roll up into enormous balls, or is that a habit only of rattlesnakes?

It is time to keep ears attuned for pinkletinks at the

Dodger Hole on the Edgartown-Vineyard Haven road. It will not be long before the Island's mute swans are comfortably nesting, except for the lonesome one in West Tisbury who still is missing a mate and seems, these days, to keep her head assiduously in the water—as if ashamed that her pulchritude has not yet succeeded in attracting a male. On Chilmark Pond, the dozen or so swans who live there have begun to pair off.

The first ladybug I have seen this season landed on a windowsill last week, and a little black house beetle got turned upside down on the porch and had to be righted.

The ground has thawed enough now to make extricating parsnips from gardens a possibility. Frost makes them succulent and sweet, but it also holds them firmly in the garden, and it is not until round about mid-March that hungry parsnip growers have access to their crops. But I have just been peeling a crisp, fresh parsnip and sautéing it in butter, and it was worth the wait.

Parsnips, which are second only to an uglifruit for unattractiveness, remind me of oysters, which have an equally ungainly shape, and oysters make me think of mussels, for which I went searching on the weekend. I learned then that March waters still are ice cold, and that mussels are so stubbornly attached to their rocks by their beards that only a craving for a soupbowl of mussels and shallots in white wine that won't be denied makes it worthwhile to contend with them.

Being suburb-bred, it is a special treat to watch a country spring, for it is so new to me. My recollections of the first signs of spring are of the pug noses—seed pods, I suppose they are—forming on maple trees and falling to the sidewalk to be squashed into cracks by roller skates. And I remember that spring was always the time—once the ground was soft enough for it—for turning over the old lawn with a garden fork and sprinkling grass seed on it—patting it down and tying strips of white cloth to a wire round the lawn patch to frighten the sparrows away.

Just as in the country, of course, it was also a time of wet earth smells and liver-colored worms.

The worms remind me of a visit to Iowa in spring two years ago. The incident is not especially relevant, except that it occurred in early April and amused me at the time. It is the only time I have ever had a solemn discussion of the qualities of worms. I'm sure if I were a fisherman I would know all about them, but in this instance, I was only trying to make friends with a grumpy desk clerk in a small town hotel. I was alone, spending a good deal of time reading bus timetables in the lobby and watching the comings and goings, not of hotel patrons as I at first thought, but of fishermen buying their worms from under the counter.

The hotel, I suspect, had long ceased doing much business in rooms—but in worms—that was something entirely different! At lunchtime, when all the worm-buying clientele seemed to have gone elsewhere, I ventured to go up to the desk clerk and ask about what he was selling.

"Why, worms," he said a bit crustily, and from under the counter he brought forth eight cans of them. Whenever a customer came in, he would take out a handful of them, slap them in a newspaper square and hand them over, only, however, after a lengthy harangue about what worm catches what fish in what pond.

Here, I am told, fishermen will soon be catching white perch at Deep Bottom. "Any day now," one optimist tells me. "They're the next fish to go after once the herring have started to run."

I have enjoyed the winter, but—as always—it has been a

long one. It is curious the way each winter seems a little bit longer by March than the one before was. And so it is good that spring is here; the air is beginning to glow and the ground to break with green shoots.

Along the King's Highway

March 26

The other morning I went out looking for the King's Highway. In the eighteenth century, I had read somewhere, J. Hector St. John de Crèvecoeur, the French salesman, surveyor and explorer who visited the colonies and described them in *Letters from an American Farmer*, had followed it. Although in a pocket edition of his book, I could find no reference to the cross-Vineyard route he had taken, there was a map there of "The Island of Martha's Vineyard and Its Dependencies," and a jiggly line stretched from Edgartown to Gay Head.

I have since learned that the jiggly line includes more than that royal route—that the King's Highway, so far as anyone knows, began only in what is now West Tisbury and meandered through Chilmark woods and fields, and probably stopped there. But after all, that is precisely where I took my walk, and since my feet were put on the right path by a student of historical matters, I have no doubt that I was walking where de Crèvecoeur found the Island's soil "light and sandy" and its inhabitants "all Presbyterians. . .without gloom, but with a decorum and reserve so natural to them that I thought myself in Philadelphia."

My walk began auspiciously, with a meeting with a friend who is a great walker and an historian, as well. I told him I was looking for the King's Highway. He nodded sagely, and told me he would show me exactly where I should go.

We crawled under a fence on the Middle Road, crossed the Tiasquin where it bubbles furiously over rocks, and then we climbed a hill. My companion said that he would leave me there—that I would know the way by wagon ruts of years, and that if I were ever uncertain which way to go when I reached a fork, I should bear right. He said the old King's Highway was now used as a riding trail, so there would be hoofprints to guide me.

The woods, just now, are showing only the faintest stirrings of spring. Here and there in a stream bed, there is the vivid purple of a skunk cabbage spathe, but no green leaves yet. Although there are snowdrops in West Tisbury dooryards, and crocuses and pinkletinks in warmer sections of the Island, the woods still are largely brown, except where arbutus leaves peek through the dead leaf carpet, or there are moss patches.

I found myself, as my path followed the winding Tiasquin, quite taken with the mosses and the lichens—there are so many of them. There was a fragile, wispy sort—a pale gray-green variety that hangs from trees in dank places—a miniature Spanish moss is what it most resembles.

Then there was something cool and chartreuse that clung to the bark of the wild cherry. On a dead limb, I admired what my guidebook tells me must have been a liverwort—but surely there is some prettier name for it! It looks so delicate and snowflake-like—as if, beneath a magnifying glass, it would have all sorts of intricate and graceful patterns.

Elsewhere, there were moss tufts speckled like pincushions. Covering a rill was a deep green moss, of a rich, royal shade that reminded me again that I was walking the King's Highway.

I came to a meadow (I am told it was David Look's goat meadow a century ago).

From the meadow, I heard the honking of geese and the still air was jabbed with duck calls. I followed the sounds and looked below to Stan Murphy's pond where a pair of Canada geese were entertaining visiting mallards.

Beyond the meadow, the path I was following did, indeed, turn into a two-rut road. A reddish brook trickled beside it, and I remembered a New Hampshire brook where, somewhat queasily, I used to pick watercress as a child. The name of that stream was Bloody Brook—so named after a battle between the Piscataquas and a neighboring tribe. Even though the battle had occurred in French and Indian War days—or before—the name could not help but make the watercress unappetizing. As it widened, the King's Highway entered the woods again. This time they were deep woods, and it was not difficult to imagine that once wagons and coaches had traveled between the tall, gray trees, farmers had shouted "Giddap" and coachmen had smartly cracked their whips.

I stood and listened for a time. The wind in the woods at this season, when there are not yet leaves to make a fragile, tinkling sound, roars like the surf caught in a conch shell.

Silver spears of trees pierced the pale blue sky. I wondered if those trees had looked down once on the rumbling of the carts and the stagecoaches. They stood as straight and tall—whatever they were—as the poplars along a French roadside. Beyond the brook, one of them creaked ominously as the March wind freshened. A woodpecker drummed furiously. Suddenly there was a crashing through the underbrush, and the white tip of a deer's tail disappeared ahead of me.

The sunlight began to flicker in clearings just then. All morning, its shafts had been coming and going, lighting the woods for an instant, then disappearing behind the clouds the way a March sun is wont to do. It glistened on the mottled red-green leaves of the Labrador tea that looks like a huckleberry but, I am told, is an evergreen. In winter, its leaves hang in a rather sleepy way, pointing downward, as if they had not yet gathered enough strength from spring to spread out perkily.

The sun illumined, too, a rock crouched on a hillside—sentinel through the centuries, I am sure, along the King's Highway. And it glinted, too, on shards of glass and pottery in an ancient bottle dump. There were pretty pieces of pottery in it—white ironstone and flowing-blue. There was some purple glass, and glass of a sky-blue shade. There was a horseshoe that I extricated with care from beneath an old harness and gingerly placed, prongs up, in a pail I had come upon. I have never owned a horseshoe before and did not want the good fortune to spill out.

I walked only a little while longer, for the woods grew deeper and the path seemed to go off in several ways, and I could find no hoofprints to follow.

The King's Highway can be entered, too, I am told, at Abel's Hill and Nab's Corner—where a house of ill repute stood centuries ago, they say. So another day, when the bell-like blooms of the huckleberry are out, and the yarrow is diffusing a spicy fragrance, and the sun has decided to stay for a while, I will go exploring on the royal route again.